Communication and Society
Editor: Jeremy Tunstall

The Fleet Street Disaster

In the same series

Journalists at work
Jeremy Tunstall

The making of a TV series
Philip Elliott
(available in the United States from Hastings House)

The political impact of mass media
Colin Seymour-Ure

The manufacture of news
Stan Cohen and Jock Young (editors)

Children in front of the small screen
Grant Noble

The silent watchdog
David Murphy

*This book is the seventh volume in a series
edited by Jeremy Tunstall and devoted to
explorations of the interrelationships between
society and all forms of communication media*

GRAHAM CLEVERLEY

The Fleet Street Disaster

British national newspapers
as a case study in mismanagement

with a preface by
REX WINSBURY

CONSTABLE
London

SAGE Publications
Beverly Hills, California

Published in Great Britain 1976
by Constable and Company Ltd
10 Orange Street, London WC2H 7EG
Hardback ISBN 0 09 460940 3
Paperback ISBN 0 09 460950 0

Published in the United States of America 1976
by Sage Publications Inc.
275 South Beverly Drive
Beverly Hills California 90212
ISBN 0–8039–9989–5
Library of Congress Catalog Card No. 76–25733

Set in Monotype Times
Printed in Great Britain by The Anchor Press Ltd
and bound by Wm Brendon & Son Ltd
both of Tiptree, Essex

Contents

Preface

by Rex Winsbury

Fleet Street is a unique sociological phenomenon, both as home of one of the largest and most diversified national presses in the world, and as scene of the most bizarre relationship between management and unions, and between product and profit, that British and perhaps European industry has to offer. Now, in 1976, reform of Fleet Street is once again in the air, with the object of preserving the size and diversity of Britain's national press by curing or alleviating the managerial and financial peculiarities that have weakened and debilitated it. There have been reform movements before, specifically in 1964 and 1970, but both foundered on the rocks of suspicion – suspicion between managements and unions, and suspicion between rival managements that prevented any united and constructive approach to the unions. Since 1973, when the research for this book was done, Fleet Street has slipped from boom to slump in its economic fortunes, with unprecedented suddenness. There have been slumps before, since Fleet Street, like the newspaper industry in general, mirrors fairly closely the cycles of the economy as a whole. But each slump has tended to be worse than the last one, and the 1974/5 depression that hit Fleet Street was sufficiently serious for the government to ask the Royal Commission on the Press, set up in mid-1974, for an 'urgent interim report' on the state of its finances. That interim report, published in March 1976, contained the table overleaf showing the dismal profits performance of the national press, and in particular of the so-called 'quality press'.

These are the grim figures that have prompted and given urgency to the latest movement towards reform of Fleet Street, for even the improvement in profit for the popular press in 1975 gives them only a wafer-thin margin for survival. It can of course be argued that there is nothing new about these financial problems – they may have got worse, but they are still fundamentally the same in character as when previous reform movements ran into the sands. Why then should this latest attempt succeed?

The answer lies in two new elements that are now present but

TRADING PROFITS EXPRESSED AS A PERCENTAGE OF TURNOVER
1970–1975

	1970	1971	1972	1973	1974	1975
Popular Dailies*	2·8	6·9	5·8	−0·2	−0·4	4·0
Quality Dailies	−3·9	2·5	7·1	2·7	−2·2	−4·8
Popular Sundays	7·7	5·6	6·2	3·6	−1·0	5·0
Quality Sundays	−2·8	−4·9	1·3	3·0	−3·2	−8·1

Source: Royal Commission on the Press.
*Including London evenings.

which were not there before to concentrate the minds of union leaders and managers. One is the arrival of totally new printing and production techniques which are causing an immense technological upheaval in the newspaper and publishing industry world-wide: these new techniques would of themselves necessitate a total reappraisal of manning and machinery in Fleet Street, as they are already doing in the American and British regional press. The second element is the recommendation by the Royal Commission in its interim report that special government aid should be available to newspapers to enable them to tackle the problems of 'new technology', this being considered the most practical way of helping them with their financial problems. State aid of this type, although hedged about and deliberately limited in scope so as to avoid charges of political interference with the freedom of the Press, nevertheless crosses a momentous watershed in British political life. For while the Press throughout Europe for many years has been subsidised by government, Britain has stood out as the main exception (West Germany, with the example of Nazi domination of the Press before it, has also tried to keep aid to its newspapers to a minimum, but even there the pressures are strong for more public money and tax relief to help the Press).

This independence from government has been a great source of pride and strength to Fleet Street, as to the British press as a whole: for with financial independence came editorial independence, and with editorial independence and large circulations came political influence and power (resented by many but universally acknowledged). This was all very well as long as financial independence was based on adequate profits to sustain it, and as long as stable or rising circulations commanded the respect of public, politicians and the advertisers who contribute so much of Fleet Street's revenue. But profits have dwindled, and as to circulations, this was the discouraging position shown by the Royal Commission, as rapidly rising cover prices bit into sales:

CIRCULATION OF NATIONAL NEWSPAPERS
AVERAGE DAILY CIRCULATION (thousands)

	1961	*1966*	*1971*	*1974*	*1975*
POPULAR DAILIES					
Daily Express	4,321	3,978	3,413	3,154	2,822
Daily Mail	2,649	2,318	1,798	1,753	1,726
Daily Mirror	4,578	5,132	4,384	4,205	3,968
Daily Sketch	991	857	—	—	—
Sun/Daily Herald	1,407	1,238	2,293	3,380	3,446
Total	13,946	13,523	11,888	12,492	11,962
QUALITY DAILIES					
Daily Telegraph	1,248	1,353	1,446	1,406	1,331
Guardian	240	281	332	359	319
Financial Times	132	152	170	195	181
The Times	257	282	340	345	319
Total	1,877	2,068	2,288	2,305	2,150
TOTAL DAILIES	15,823	15,591	14,176	14,797	14,112
POPULAR SUNDAYS					
News of the World	6,689	6,152	6,129	5,824	5,479
Sunday Express	4,113	4,181	4,108	4,015	3,715
Sunday Mirror/					
Pictorial	5,320	5,219	4,683	4,576	4,251
Sunday People/					
The People	5,446	5,560	4,852	4,387	4,188
Total	21,568	21,112	19,772	18,802	17,633
QUALITY SUNDAYS					
Observer	722	881	799	819	730
Sunday Citizen/					
Reynolds News	318	216	—	—	—
Sunday Telegraph	688	650	755	777	752
Sunday Times	994	1,363	1,418	1,478	1,380
Total	2,722	3,110	2,972	3,074	2,862
TOTAL SUNDAYS	24,290	24,222	22,744	21,876	20,495

In other words, during 1974 and 1975 both the sales and the cash position of Fleet Street had been seriously undermined, to the point where worries about the future of certain titles, though not new, intensified sufficiently to overcome the traditional antipathy, on both sides, to government aid to the Press. As for 1976, the Royal Commission in March forecast that the quality press would have an adverse cash outflow of £8 million, with the popular press slightly worse off than in 1975, and the London evening papers making even higher losses. 'We are satisfied that 1976 will be a third successive year of loss for a number of houses', it wrote in its report.

The remedy it proposed was that the government should in effect act as lender of last resort to those newspaper companies which could not otherwise afford the cost of investing in new technology and of buying out the labour which the new technology would make redundant. For it saw as the only route to at least temporary salvation the dramatic savings in labour costs that can be achieved with the rational introduction of new technology (by 'new technology' is meant a bundle of new word-processing, type-setting and plate-making processes which centre on the use of the computer to do the main time-consuming jobs of storage and arrangement of text and advertisements, ready for high-speed photographic creation of the actual columns of text for the newspaper).

The Royal Commission estimated that the total cost to Fleet Street of investing in the new equipment and paying off perhaps a third of its labour force (up to a half in certain critical departments) might be about £50-55 million: but the annual savings on labour costs thereafter might be as high as £35 million – a very handsome return on the initial investment, if only you can afford that investment.

The trouble was that some companies could not afford it, and were not in a stable enough financial position to borrow the money, even with such an attractive potential return. So while those companies which still had a reasonable basis for borrowing should turn for loans to a normal commercial institution like Finance for Industry, said the Royal Commission, those that could not do so should be able to borrow from the government: and as an additional sweetener the government should offer interest relief to all companies which borrowed money, from whatever source, for new technology.

This last addition to the package of aid was put in as much to prove to the unions that the government was in earnest about seeking reform of Fleet Street, as to act as a pure financial inducement to managements (whose gains were clear enough anyway). Whether the government would accept these recommendations was still not decided when this book went to press: it took note of the Commission's findings, but said that before making up its mind it would await detailed reports from the companies about their financial needs.

But a much more fundamental question was whether, state aid or no state aid, Fleet Street was in any position to reform itself: and it is here that the evidence produced in this book becomes central to the whole argument. For only by understanding the full peculiarities of Fleet Street can one understand what needs reforming, how to reform it, and how difficult reform may be. What this book tells is how Fleet Street got itself into the mess that it is undoubtedly in, and what the elements of that mess are. In the new context of reform with the (to some extent accidental) conjunction of economic crisis, new technology, and the chance of outside financial assistance, Fleet Street has to pick its way gingerly out of the minefield that is mapped out, sector by sector, in this book.

Until quite recently, there was little published information about the detailed state of labour relations and management competence in Fleet Street, although there have long been more or less wild generalisations floating around about the level of earnings of printing workers and their power to 'stop the paper' if their demands were not met. But now that gap is being remedied. In 1975 there was published a valuable if rather formalised analysis of the structure and sources of earnings in Fleet Street (*Industrial Relations in Fleet Street*, by Keith Sisson, Basil Blackwell), and then the Royal Commission itself published some useful estimates of how many workers would be made redundant by the introduction of new technology – about 7,000 out a total of 20,000 production workers, plus some casuals.

This is a very high proportion, and what is hard to estimate is how many of these men are, on a strict definition of need, really 'needed' even with the existing technology (which is nearly 100 years old, being based on a series of Victorian inventions using molten metal to form the type and the printing plates). But it is certain that Fleet Street has suffered from a high degree of over-manning for many years, and that the arrival of new technology is simply the necessary catalyst to bring about the re-examination of manning levels that ought to have taken place anyway.

But the great contribution of this book is that it spells out in detail the shop floor labour practices, and the managerial sins of omission and commission, that have brought about the often astonishing state of affairs in Fleet Street's employment system. It therefore adds flesh to the bare bones of the other analyses. Having been involved in Fleet Street management for five years, after a period as a journalist, and then being given the freedom of a year's research, the author has put together a colourful, almost Damon Runyonesque account of the (almost literally) twilight world of the printing works, with its private Runyonesque language ('blow', 'fat', 'ghost workers', not to mention more formal expressions like 'chapel' and 'Imperial Father') and Runyonesque situations where, for example, a man works for two different companies at once but forgets what false name he was using at the second one so cannot collect his pay packet.

This ground level description of what is in effect a world apart, where normal rational standards simply do not apply, is however only part of the book. The rest is an attack, the more telling because it is the more difficult to do unless you have been 'on the inside', on the standards and attitudes of management in Fleet Street. The charge made against Fleet Street's managers is, in essence, that they failed to recognise the role of profit in running a newspaper, as any other commercial enterprise: that they failed to make a proper analysis of the financial mechanics of running a newspaper, so that they pursued advertising for advertising's sake, without realising the true cost of doing so: that they failed to recognise the true responsibilities of the various managers, in particular giving the advertising manager high status and the circulation manager low status, and not recognising at all the role of the editor of the newspaper as chief marketing manager: and that they surrendered control of the production process to the unions, so turning what in most other industries is an employment relationship into what can most nearly be described as a 'sub-contracting' relationship, in which the unions agree to produce the newspaper in return for certain specified payments and job guarantees.

It is fair to add that since this analysis was written events have moved on somewhat. A more professional type of manager is appearing, and the threat to jobs posed by the new technology has brought managements and unions round the same table again to discuss in a more objective way how to tackle the financial and labour problems of the industry. There now appears to be a general recognition of the need for a 'spring clean' of management and union attitudes, although it may take time to see how far these intentions translate into practice. Also, some companies have been making a consistent, long-term effort to bring order into their employment situation, with some success although still leaving far to go.

But the fundamentals of the situation are as this book says – that managements must be clear as never before about their commercial and financial objectives (and not, for example, pursue the great god of circulation at the expense of everything else), while unions must accept that they are now operating in a harsher, more exacting environment where the old rules and assumptions about how far it was permissible to 'take weak managements to the cleaners' no longer apply. The best hope lies in another feature pointed out in this book – the very real commitment to the industry felt by most people who work in it, at all levels.

But, when all is said and done, is it an industry that it is worth being committed to? Is it worth spending taxpayers' money on propping it up or putting it back on its financial feet? The sceptics fall into two groups. There are those who see it is a 'capitalist press', reactionary in tone and influence, which is best left to crumble under the weight of its own internal contradictions: it would be no loss, and with any luck a new press might arise that more truly reflected the needs and interests of the people rather than the proprietors.

The other group argue that, financially, Fleet Street is doomed anyway, because the money that has in the past supported it is switching elsewhere. The table overleaf from the Royal Commission report tells the story.

With advertising revenue swinging away from national newspapers and magazines to regional and local publications, it is argued, the future lies with the provincial press, and money would be better spent refurbishing the better regional papers rather than helping 'lame ducks' in Fleet Street (that applies both to taxpayers' money and to the money spent by the companies themselves in subsidising their Fleet Street operations out of their provincial profits).

There is strength in both arguments – we do not have a satisfactory national press, even if it is better than most countries have, and the provincial press should wake up more to the new social responsibilities that its relative financial prosperity brings with it. Equally, there is little case for an indefinite guarantee of life for Fleet Street at the taxpayers' expense: to hold out that prospect is to turn Fleet Street

SHARE OF DIFFERENT MEDIA IN TOTAL ADVERTISING EXPENDITURE, 1960–1974
(Percentage of Total)

	1960	1964	1968	1970	1971	1972	1973	1974
MEDIA								
National newspapers	19·8	20·7	19·7	19·5	18·3	18·4	18·3	17·9
Regional newspapers	23·8	23·6	24·1	25·8	25·7	26·5	29·3	30.3
Magazines and periodicals	12·4	11·1	9·9	9·2	9·1	8·5	8·2	7·9
Trade and Technical Journals	9·6	8·9	9·1	9·6	8·8	8·6	8·4	8·9
Other publications	0·6	0·7	1·6	2·0	2·2	2·1	1·9	1·8
Press production costs	4·6	4·3	4·6	6·1	6·6	6·2	5·3	5·3
ALL PRESS	70·9	69·3	69·0	72·2	70·7	70·3	71·4	72·1
Television	22.3	24·5	25·6	22.6	24·2	24·9	24·0	22·6
Poster and transport	5·0	4·3	4·0	3·9	3·9	3·7	3·5	3·8
Cinema	1·5	1·4	1·2	1·1	1·0	1·0	0·8	0·9
Radio	0·3	0·5	0·2	0·2	0·2	0·1	0·2	0·7
ALL MEDIA	100	100	100	100	100	100	100	100

Source: The Advertising Association.

into a permanent pensioner and dependant of government, which is certainly to be avoided.

But just because the idiocies and fallacies and sins of Fleet Street are so glaring and so pronounced, it is surely worth one final attempt, primed if necessary with public money, to sort out the mess and see what the true basic cost of a national press is, given the use of up-to-date technology and intelligent management. If, when the computers are in and the managers and unions have done their best or worst to produce a more expertly organised industry, the prospects for survival are still dim, then titles will have to be allowed to die, without regret or sentiment. The more difficult decision will then be where to draw the line – speaking hypothetically, would you allow *The Times* and *The Guardian* to die, or not?

Meanwhile, there is something practical that can be done to help the situation, and to give at least a new lease of life to an institution that has undeniably played, and still plays, a central part in British political and social life. The basic task is surely to improve Fleet Street's performance rather than tamely to allow it to perish. In 1976 the talk is all about 'new technology' as the way to tackle the problem. But it is important to realise that this is merely the way into the circle, the point of entry into the maze of managerial, financial, editorial and union cul-de-sacs in which Fleet Street has lost its way. In mapping out that maze, with the benefit of both direct managerial experience and personal research, this book may help to avert the final Fleet Street disaster.

Introduction

That much publicised Fleet Street event, the scoop, is not so common in real life as in fiction. Nevertheless, it is hardly rare. But the scoop that Peter Jenkins, the industrial correspondent of *The Guardian*, produced for his paper in the autumn of 1966 was unique. For while *The Guardian* was the only paper to carry the story, its contents were already known in every board-room in Fleet Street – and for that matter in the headquarters of every Fleet Street union.

The scoop was a detailed account of some of the conclusions of a report by the Economist Intelligence Unit (EIU) which had been commissioned by the Joint Board for the National Newspaper Industry (a union-management body) to carry out 'a comprehensive survey of the structure and operations of the industry'. By the autumn of 1966, the study had been completed, and delivered to its sponsors, who, whatever their other opinions of its contents, were at one in believing it ought not to be published. Almost at one, that is. One director of one newspaper company felt differently. After some struggle with his conscience, he leaked the report to Peter Jenkins: subsequently, he had to be persuaded by his friends not to resign.

With their hands forced, the Joint Board changed their minds. The full report was made publicly available. But the EIU had done a good job in more ways than one. The published report ran to 650-odd typewritten pages, nearly a quarter of them full-page charts and tables, and weighed over four pounds. Even at forty-five shillings a copy, it wasn't likely to be widely read, even in Fleet Street, and it wasn't.

So that the fears of the publicity-shy members of the Joint Board were not realised. No shareholders' ginger-groups were elected, even in those companies where the shareholding is wide enough for it to matter. The unions, content that management had done all it could to keep the report quiet, did not respond to the publication as another move in the endless game of ploy and counter-ploy which is labour relations in Fleet Street. No heads rolled (nobody found out who leaked the report): in general, the sky did not fall in.

And within a few weeks, the industry could lapse safely back into the private and proper obscurity it normally enjoys as the only industry not subject to the fear of public exposure. In some companies, a genuine attempt was being made at the time to improve the quality of management: there, publication of the report had been welcomed as a possible way of inducing the trauma without which no major change in managerial style is ever possible. But even there the EIU report was fairly quickly recognised to have been a non-event, dismissible by those it criticised as uninformed – and welcomed by those it faintly praised as demonstrating that, whatever *was* wrong, it was not their fault.

Thus there passed one of the very few occasions on which it seemed the veil that normally covers the working of Fleet Street management might be lifted: as it similarly passed after the publication of the reports of the Royal Commissions on the Press in 1948 and 1962, and the report of the Prices and Incomes Board in 1970.

Apart from those incidents, the obscurity has remained decent and undisturbed. A corner is sometimes lifted when a newspaper dies, but even then the attention is normally fairly closely restricted to the circumstances of the unfortunate company. Even during the turmoil that surrounded the takeover of the International Publishing Corporation (IPC) in 1970, the attention of the rest of the Press was mainly focused on the group's non-newspaper activities. The spotlight that cyclically illuminates the motor-car and other industries by and large leaves Fleet Street undisturbed. The management of Fleet Street, that is. For it is probably true that more is written about newspapers than about any other industry, save perhaps television, pop music and the other entertainment media. Books, both fiction and documentary, abound. Television is at least as concerned with the doings of the Press as it is with any other industry. Politicians are a constant source of criticisms of the way the Press is controlled – criticisms which are guaranteed their share of editorial space, since newspapers are prepared to accept that their affairs are worthy of attention.

But such exposure is limited to the necessarily public side of the industry: its editorial style and content. On that, Fleet Street is willing to expound at length. But as for the details of its private life it has the same preference as other industries for privacy, and more power to achieve it. Not that *Private Eye*-ish allegations of conspiracy to hush things up have much in them. Something may be, but not much. As

Peter Jenkins and *The Guardian* proved, editorial independence really does mean enough in some papers to allow the publishing of material that proprietors and managements would much rather see kept private. But there are factors operating that make such conspiracy unnecessary.

First among them must be the surprising lack of knowledge about the workings of their own industry possessed by most journalists. This is more a matter of choice than incapacity. Journalists on the whole represent the brightest segment of the annual intake of recruits into the industry, but most of them are inclined to shun the whole matter of managing newspapers as being slightly unworthy of them . . . with much the air of a barrister referring the question of fees to his clerk. For them the subject is a closed book which they would much rather not open: with the result that when they do write about Fleet Street affairs they tend either to perpetuate hoary old myths about the industry (like British newspapers are so cheap because they are subsidised by advertising), or to adumbrate transiently fashionable ones (like the unions are bleeding the industry to death, commercial television is stealing its advertising, and so on).

Maybe not so much in print (except in *Private Eye*, *The Socialist Worker* and a few other places) but certainly in private, otherwise quite acute journalists are even likely to claim that the industry suffers from profit-hungry and cost-conscious managements – despite the fact that it is singularly difficult to find anyone in Fleet Street who displays the least sign of being eager for profits. (Which is hardly surprising, since anyone who was looking for profits would have left the industry speedily sometime after 1955.)

Moreover, there is an understandable reluctance among editors and journalists to criticise, publicly at least, people whom they recognise as colleagues, in the sense that they meet them every day, lunch with them, join with them in meetings, and (at least for the production journalists) sometimes have common job interests. Public and overt criticism of one's colleagues is a serious breach of taboo in any industry: it is not surprising that journalists and editors refrain from it too.

These natural tendencies towards reticence are helped by the fear that to write of the economics of Fleet Street is necessarily to be concerned with labour relations; and to write of Fleet Street labour relations is to risk punitive actions by the unions. Thus, while the National Graphical Association (NGA), at one level the most pro-

fessionally conscientious of the Fleet Street unions, officially considers that it has no right to interfere with the content of newspapers,
it nevertheless reserves the right to support any member or group of
members who refuse to handle any material on grounds of conscience.
NATSOPA (National Society of Operative Printers and Assistants)
takes the matter further, and in the past has flatly refused to allow
material critical of the unions to appear. Indeed, in an ultimatum to
one paper, the general secretary of NATSOPA insisted, under threat of
industrial action, on the publication in full of a statement by him,
even though it contained patent libels on third parties, for which the
newspaper would have been liable.

To write seriously of management matters is therefore to risk
rocking the union boat: a risk editors are understandably unwilling
to run.

Finally, the situation can be rationalised, and is, by the belief that
after all, compared to questions of editorial content, questions of the
competence of management are essentially unimportant, or un-
newsworthy, or both. Conscience is thereby salved.

Ironically enough, newspaper managements are frequently ready
to bewail public ignorance of the state of affairs in their business.
'If only people knew . . .' or, more specifically, 'If only Parliament
knew . . .', they tend to say whenever there is glib left-wing talk of the
power and riches of the Press 'barons', or government legislation
like the Industrial Relations Act fails to take account of the 'special
circumstances' of the industry. By definition, if the people and
Parliament don't know, it can only be their fault. (Still, other
industries often make the same complaint. And it doesn't make them
over-eager to have Press reporters probing their affairs.)

But while they may be correct about the newsworthiness of newspaper management, to say that it is unimportant is a crucial mistake,
for two reasons, one industrial, one socio-political. From the industrial point of view, the mistake arose from the assumption that newspapers are in some critical sense different from other industries (even
that British national newspapers are crucially different from any
other kind), and that, therefore, there are no relevant lessons to be
learned from their problems.

At the drop of a pin, newspaper managements (and journalists)
will point out that they have social commitments that other industries
do not have (*pace* General Motors and Ralph Nader); that their
product is uniquely perishable (*pace* the dairy industry and the air-

lines); that they exist in a uniquely hostile union environment (*pace* any industry based on Merseyside or Clydeside). And the rest of the industrial world takes their word for it. Daintily withdrawing from possible contamination, managers in other industries avert their eyes and stop their ears: there is nothing to be learnt from studying British newspapers.

In a way, the attitude is not very different from that of Europeans who claim there is nothing to be learned from studying British labour relations. And it is just as wrong. For while the national newspaper industry, like British labour relations, may be diseased, it is from the study of diseased tissue, not the healthy kind, that most medical advances come.

From the social and political point of view, the importance of the subject lies in the assumption that society benefits from a free and varied press – an assumption that is rather fundamental to the western way of life. And while that assumption remains true, then it remains vital that the newspaper industry stay (or become again) economically healthy. If the Press is to perform its role, if journalists are to be able to carry out the 'important' part of their vocation, then it is essential that newspaper management be efficient and effective.

The 1966 EIU report forecast that by the end of the decade, three national dailies and one national Sunday paper would disappear. They were wrong mostly because some proprietors were willing to disprove further their 'hunger' for profits by continuing to keep loss-makers alive. Partly too they were wrong because Rupert Murdoch managed to do what the vaunted expertise of the International Publishing Corporation had failed to do: make a viable proposition out of *The Sun*. In so doing however he drove the *Daily Mirror*, once the solid money-spinner on which the IPC empire was built, into loss: for the first time in modern history at least, the price rise which the *Mirror* applied for in the autumn of 1973 was needed to put the paper into the black.

While they were proved wrong, therefore, the EIU forecasters weren't so far out: it is an even bet that another investigation based on the same premises would come to the same conclusion again.

In his introduction to that EIU report, Lord Devlin, Chairman of the Joint Board, was at pains to point out that that is a serious situation for society at large: if I did not agree, I would not have written this book. But he finished his introduction: 'This report does not raise problems for the press alone to solve. It raises problems also for a free democracy.'

That may be true: but the implication that in some way it is the duty of society to come to the rescue of the Press is a different matter. It is not easy to see how it could (Lord Devlin was essentially arguing for an increase in cover prices; cover prices have gone up by some 200 per cent since then and it hasn't helped much) but even if it could help, the public has a right to an accounting – especially from an industry that can pay its unskilled workers four and five thousand pounds a year, and takes upon itself the right to comment on other people's performance.

This book is an attempt to lift the veil that at the moment prevents such an accounting. It necessarily makes much use of the few previous investigations in the field: the EIU, the Royal Commissions, the Prices and Incomes Board, and two or three stockbrokers' reports. I also owe a debt to the European Institute of Business Administration for the grant which enabled me to spend a great deal of 1973 investigating in particular the state of labour relations in the industry. Otherwise it is very much the fruit of the five years I spent with the International Publishing Corporation with the overt brief of attempting to improve its management, and of the previous ten during which, admittedly, as a working journalist I suffered from much of the voluntary blindness to the business of newspapers that I have already described.

Apart from that, I owe a great deal to the many friends and colleagues in Fleet Street with whom I have argued out many of the conclusions: and to the various consultants and academics here and in the USA whose help I have often sought. Without their insights and experiences, I doubt that the book would have been possible.

1
Profits

A few years ago, at the height of the boom in management consultancy and training, I brought together for lunch an entrepreneurially-minded friend with money to invest and a couple of management consultants with interests in training, on the basis that they might find an opportunity for fruitful collaboration. It didn't work out. For, to fill a lull in the conversation, my entrepreneur friend happened to ask what consultancy fad the others saw following the then current one for behavioural science. It was an unfortunate remark; or at least an ill-chosen phrase. For at least one of the consultants went deep red at the suggestion that there was anything 'faddy' about management consultancy – or indeed that consultancy was ever motivated by anything other than the desire to improve clients' profitability.

It was I suppose an understandable reaction. My friend had transgressed one of the consultant's most cherished taboos. There wouldn't be much point in remembering the incident now, except that essentially he was right; the now-fashionable preoccupation of those departments of consultancies concerned with new product development is the question of social responsibility.

There are of course many reasons for the increasing preoccupation of managements in a wide range of industries with social responsibility: none of them are particularly my concern. What is, is that the problems that are only recently being forced upon the managers of most industries are old hat to those responsible for running newspapers.

The charge that newspaper proprietors pay too much attention to profits and too little to their public responsibilities is an ancient one. The major charge launched by both left- and right-wing critics of the Press, it goes back to the earliest days of the emergence of newspapers in the eighteenth century, and is so widespread that examples are hardly worth quoting. Though it may just be worth noting that to begin with such criticism was virtually entirely right-wing. The distaste felt by Trollope's protagonists for the machinations of Quintus Slide is typical of the reaction of an established class with the feeling that making money is its own prerogative, and one that it should be able to exercise in private. It isn't until the arrival of a left-wing establishment that the same charge is launched from the other side.

In both cases, however, the charge that the Press will go to 'any lengths' to make money usually implies that it is attacking the person making the charge, or someone associated with him.

But the charge of excessive concern with profits is also made by another, perhaps less biased group – journalists themselves. Most books about the Press are written by journalists. Their overwhelming concern therefore is with editorial quality; and their overriding message is that quality and responsibility are damaged by excessive attention to making money. The charge is not only launched against managements that deliberately alter editorial policy in order to increase profits. It is even made against those proprietors, like Gordon Newhouse in the United States or Lord Thomson internationally, whose pride is that they never interfere with editorial matters. (As a typical example of such slightly muddled accusations, see Francis Williams's *The Right to Know, passim.*)

At a more mundane level, complaints about the profit-consciousness of 'management' is a continuing and constant theme of journalists' conversation. Given half a chance to unburden themselves, most journalists have at their fingertips an impressive list of instances in which they or their stories, or their friends' stories, suffered at the hands of a miserly commercial management. I have even heard it suggested (by a talented and famous journalist who really ought to have known better) that the reason for the decline of the International Publishing Corporation in the late 'sixties and early 'seventies was that it 'had fallen into the hands of the accountants': whereas from my own experience there the allegation that any kind of effective financial control was ever exercised by IPC over its newspapers is the purest kind of fable.

Still, if we take the evidence of politicians of left and right, add it to the complaints of the journalists, and couple them with public opinion as it tends to be expressed in the higher-brow weeklies, the picture that emerges of Fleet Street is of yet another industry where concern for profit has been allowed to operate against the public good.

Unfortunately for that picture, the view from other quarters has been different. In 1968, Aubrey Jones, then head of the Prices and Incomes Board (PIB), expressed privately his surprise about the tactics of IPC on cover prices. Some while before, Cecil King, the Chairman of IPC, had approached the PIB for an increase of one penny on the *Daily Mirror*'s price. His argument had been that, if the *Mirror* was not allowed to raise its price, no other popular paper would be able to do so. The *Daily Mirror* (in those days) didn't need the extra money, but the other papers did. So unless the *Mirror*'s increase was allowed, the others would be in trouble and some might even fold.

Aubrey Jones didn't challenge the argument: in fact the increase was granted. What he did do was point out that in those circumstances the action of a profit-motivated company would be to hold its prices down and if possible force its rivals out of business. The IPC argument may have been an honourable one; it was not the argument of a company bent on maximising its own profits.

Similarly, the terms on which IPC some time later, not under Cecil King, sold *The Sun* to Rupert Murdoch were not those that any profit-oriented proprietor would ever have agreed to. And the millions of pounds that the Thomson Organisation has sunk into its rescue operation at *The Times* (after eight years it is still a rescue operation) was hardly an expenditure likely to commend itself to anyone with a hard nose for profits. Which may be why for many years the resultant losses were carefully kept out of the Thomson Organisation accounts by charging them to a separate family company, while keeping dividends up for outside shareholders by having family shareholders pass theirs.

All these acts could of course have been the result of pure incompetence: but to believe so strains credulity unbearably (though it is the theory most widely held among Fleet Street union members). There undoubtedly was a fair amount of incompetence involved, but the simpler and more likely explanation is that in each case the dominating motive was not profit, but the desire, for whatever reason, to keep the titles alive.

Moreover, to put against the politicians' and the journalists' views there are those of two other significant groups. One group I have just mentioned: the trade unions. While it is true that most union members, as I will be describing more fully later, believe firmly in the incompetence of Fleet Street management, they are also usually prepared to assert that profitability is one of the last things those managements think about. (At least they do so in private: in public the ones with political careers to think about are reasonably careful to maintain the attack on capitalist control of the industry.) Not, of course, that they are prepared to concede altruism or public service any important place among management motives. The chief contenders, in their view, are: 'an easy life'; 'prestige'; 'impressing the other members of their clubs'; 'keeping the family happy'; and so on. Or, less commonly but in some ways more charitably, they will assert that newspapers are deliberately run at a loss so that profits will accrue to other parts of a group enterprise (making newsprint, printing, running advertising agencies, and the like). The last charge smacks a little of paranoia. But the first, that quite a number of things concern Fleet Street managements rather more than making money, is also borne out by the second significant group: the outsiders who began to move into some areas of management in the industry in the 'sixties.

From something like 1965 onward (the time of the 'white-hot technological revolution' when 'management' was good, growth was great and the Stock Market was beginning to boom) some of the more outward-looking Fleet Street organisations (notably IPC and Thomson) began to recruit people from outside the industry in order to improve the way they were managed. It didn't eventually make a great deal of difference (on the newspaper side of the organisations anyway) and the inward flow fairly soon reversed itself with the happy consent of both parties.

But in the intervening period, the years of good intentions that followed the EIU report, a number of plans were laid, some of them perhaps grandiose but most of them sensible, for transforming what Stafford Beer (now a professor at the Open University, but then IPC's Director of Development) characterised as a 'machine built for running downhill' into one with at least some capacity for climbing. But the mistake generally made was to assume that the managements the plans were being made for wanted to go uphill; wanted, that is, to increase profits. Maybe at one level they did. But the lesson that most of the 'reformers' of that epoch carry with them still is that there are several things that Fleet Street managers put at a higher level than improving profits. Different people's memories give them different degrees of importance, but constantly among them are:

—building a bigger circulation than your rival
—increasing the volume of advertising (preferably to more than your rival's)
—achieving any kind of coup which arouses the professional admiration of the rest of the industry

—ensuring that nothing happens to question the validity of the professional qualifications of the people involved

And, above all, looking good. Or, more accurately perhaps, making senior management or the proprietor feel good.

Now, unfortunately for profits, what makes most people feel good is not making money, but spending it. The major appeal of the *Mirror* Magazine (of which much more later) to the IPC management was that it was a major breakthrough, and a splendid achievement: in short, that it cost money. The same must have been true of the introduction of colour advertising into the *Daily Express*, since for years and years they only carried it at a loss. And, looking at the cases of, say, the *Sunday Telegraph* and *The Times*, the only choice of motivations that one can ascribe to their proprietors for continuing with them is between sheer altruism and simple pride of possession.

It doesn't take much investigation for it to become quickly apparent that the popular picture of capitalist entrepreneurs perverting the purpose of the Press for the sake of profits is considerably wide of the mark. Just as wide of the mark however would be the assertion that the national newspapers are managed altruistically in the service of the people and their need for information. Which is, oddly enough, an assertion that *is* sometimes made, though usually only in speeches at internal gatherings and in publications like the near-masterpiece of mutual adulation published to raise funds for the new Press Club, and called, simply, *Fleet Street*. (Which is not something that should be missed by anyone with a taste for dramatic irony. It also contains such choice plums as a laudatory profile by Sir Hugh Cudlipp of Cecil King, the boss he was shortly to replace; and an article carefully outlining the management changes that had taken place to strengthen *The Times,* a matter of months before it had to be sold to Thomson.)

The truth of the matter is that Fleet Street suffers neither from too single-minded a devotion to profit, nor from dedication to the public service at the expense of profit. What it suffers from is a congenital disability to understand what its purpose *is*, even at the top of the organisation.

It also suffers, generally, from a congenital disability to recognise its confusion. A number of ready-to-wear formulas are always at hand for any company that wants to parrot a statement of purpose without going to the trouble of thinking it through, and Fleet Street managements are as ready as those of other industries to trot them out: the difference being that whereas in other industries the formula tends to mask a fairly clear idea of what the organisation is actually trying to do, in Fleet Street it only masks uncertainty.

The difficulty is also enhanced in Fleet Street by the industry's general hyper-sensitivity to public relations and the right 'image', coupled with the realisation that anything decided in any Fleet Street board-room is likely to become fairly public knowledge in a matter of days. The reaction of senior Fleet Street managements to a request for a statement of long-term purpose by, say, a group of corporate planners wanting to get their teeth into something to work with, is immediately and disastrously tinged by the desire to find a formula that will sound good.

This only adds to the difficulties that people in industry in general have with the clarification of objectives: the feeling that if you tell people what you're after, you give them a weapon to use against you; reluctance to spend time formulating basic objectives when 'everyone knows what we're doing anyway'; and, sometimes, a dislike of cant, hypocrisy and pretentiousness coupled with the belief that other people's statements of purpose are canting, hypocritical and pretentious.

This general lack of clarity of purpose is thrown into sharper relief by the few exceptions. In 1948, Lord Beaverbrook, in his evidence to the Royal Commission on the Press, left no doubts about what his primary purpose was: the achievement of political influence and power. The making of an adequate profit was only a secondary objective necessary (in normal circumstances) for the fulfilment of the first. Equally clear, in conversation anyway, is the management of *The Guardian*, which at least since the 'twenties hasn't been trying to make a profit at all, and clearly sees its editorial purpose as the primary one. That is why the organisation bought *The Manchester Evening News* in the late 'twenties: to provide the profits on which *The Guardian* could survive. It is also why *The Guardian* (but not *The Manchester Evening News*) determines the size of its edition each day not by the amount of advertising available, but by editorial demand. That is, the amount of editorial space necessary to record the events of the day (and comment on them) is determined on purely editorial criteria; and it is provided irrespective of the amount of advertising space there is available to support it.

But Beaverbrook is dead; and, apart from *The Guardian*, the only place in Fleet Street nowadays where one senses any clarity of purpose is in the offices of News International. The pragmatic single-mindedness of the Murdoch organisation frequently leads to a certain amount of unpopularity with the rest of the industry (as, in June 1974, when it immediately conceded a claim from SOGAT [Society of Graphic and Allied Trades] in its provincial offices that was threatening a Fleet Street close-down, without going through any of the ritual posturings usually considered necessary). But it has also made it Fleet Street's nearest approach to a success story in modern times.

Elsewhere, uncertainty about the place of profit in a newspaper's objectives is confounded with confusion about what makes a newspaper profitable: in particular with confusion between increasing sales and increasing profits. And the result of the confusion worse confounded is the sorry economic record of Fleet Street in the last twenty years (roughly speaking, and significantly, since the end of newsprint rationing). The list of closures during that period is familiar and painful enough to barely warrant mentioning. But in case anyone has forgotten there used to be a *News Chronicle*, a *Star*, a *Sketch*, and a *Herald* published every day, and an *Empire*(!) *News*, a *Citizen*, a *Despatch*, and a *Graphic* published every Sunday.

That, apart from those, the *Sunday Telegraph* and *The Guardian* would already have been closed by anyone seriously trying to make money, I have already mentioned. Much the same is true of *The Observer*, where the management has a clearer-than-average concept that it isn't really trying to make profits, or at least not much, so that they'll keep going unless the bailiffs actually move in.

Probably *The Times* (which oddly enough didn't actually lose money until Thomson's took it over, though it was heading that way) is in the same category, though it would conflict with the hard-headed Thomson image to admit it. Among the other dailies, the *Express*, the *Mail* and the *Mirror* are all flirting dangerously with the red ink; though the *Mail* and the *Mirror* can probably depend on continuing support from more profitable associates, the *Express* can probably do no more than continue to lop off the more serious drains on its resources (like the late *Scottish Daily Express*). *The Sun*, while on absolute figures it would probably have to be considered dicey, can at least look hopefully at its trends: in the tabloid battle *The Sun* is still gaining and the *Mirror* still losing.

A parallel battle still carries on in the mass end of the Sunday market though from the point of view of titles if not owners the fight is a three-cornered one between IPC's *Mirror* and *People* and Murdoch's *News of the World*. Which leaves the four reasonably healthy-looking papers. The *Sunday Express*, however, may not be sound enough to continue to support the daily edition, while the *Sunday Times*, like most fat people, is not so healthy as it looks. The weight penalty it carries is likely to be increasingly dangerous in an era of escalating newsprint prices.

The Financial Times, on the other hand, rests on a bedrock of financial and business advertising, while the *Daily Telegraph* appears equally firmly based on the need of the middle-class for a channel for small advertising and reinforcement of its political and social attitudes. (Nevertheless, and less tangibly, the *Daily Telegraph* does tend to suffer from the same kind of smug conviction of its own superiority that used to afflict the *Daily Mirror* before the arrival of the new *Sun*: the *Telegraph* could be just as vulnerable to the same kind of attack, were there a credible attacker around.)

It hasn't been overlooked by commentators that the few healthy newspapers in that list are all in dominant, near-monopoly positions in their particular market segments. Many people have therefore jumped to the 'obvious' conclusion that the ultimate end of present trends will be three daily and three Sunday papers, one of each in the quality, middle-brow, and popular fields. It is an obvious conclusion, but there are reasons for considering it less than certain, quite apart from the fact that one of its leading proponents used to be Cecil King.

There are two reasons for doubting it: one is that monopoly is not sufficient to guarantee survival, and the other that monopoly is not necessary to ensure it. On the first count there are easily enough examples of loss-making monopolies around in other industries to indicate that something is wrong with the theory. Monopoly only becomes profitable when it is associated with (a) a continuing, active demand for the product; (b) political freedom to set prices in the most advantageous way; and (c) managerial and productive efficiency great enough to ensure that costs are lower than the price the market will bear.

Two of those (a and c) are completely independent of the degree of monopoly in the situation; and, in modern circumstances, the second, freedom to set prices, is probably inversely related to monopoly – the greater the degree of monopoly the greater the likelihood of governmental control over price (and quality). Indeed, once monopoly positions are established, then the most powerful argument for the preservation of a private enterprise Press – that it ensures variety of expressed opinion – disappears. The result of a market-segment-monopoly solution might well be nationalisation, BBC-style. And it is a moot point whether such nationalisation could fairly be called 'survival'.

Apart from nationalisation, however, the profitability of a monopoly still depends on continuing demand and productive efficiency: but if those two things can be achieved – if people still want newspapers, and they can be produced more effectively and cheaply than now – then the need for monopoly disappears. Which is the second of the two arguments against the market-segment-monopoly outcome. Put another way, if one truly extrapolates demand and productivity trends, you don't end up with monopoly newspapers but with no newspapers at all. For a while you may reach a period of high-circulation papers, fat with advertising: but the assumptions that high circulation and high advertising volume equates with profitability is a cherished Fleet Street myth that has little foundation in fact.

I shall be exploring those myths in more detail later. For the moment however it is worth a passing look at some of the alternatives to the market-segment-monopoly solution that have been proposed.

The Royal Commission on the Press of 1962, unlike its 1948 predecessor which was called to consider how the power of the Press could be controlled, was concerned with how the Press could be helped to survive without a monopoly. Of the several suggestions made to it, two have had a certain survival value and have re-emerged in recent months, so they are worth looking at again, even though the 1962 Commission quite rightly rejected them. The first, perhaps an obvious one, is that rich newspapers should be made to subsidise poor ones. From a theoretical point of view this would mean extending to the whole industry the principle that already exists within newspaper groups (the *Telegraph–Sunday Telegraph* or *Sunday Times–Times* symbiosis, for example). From a practical point of view however it has flaws, whichever of the two basic forms it takes: redistribution of a tax on profits or a tax on revenue.

Either way, the proposal rests on the basic and somewhat shaky assumption that the rich papers make enough money to cover the losses of the poor ones: if that isn't true, long-term, the net result would only be that everyone goes bust slowly instead of some quickly.

But even if it is true, each of the two forms of redistribution have side-effects which tend to negate their usefulness. Thus, if it is profit that is taxed, there can be no guarantee that the recipient company will use the money to reduce losses. In the present state of the industry, a much more likely outcome is that the money will be utilised to make the newspaper more 'competitive' – i.e., to increase its costs through, for instance, producing bigger papers, producing more editions, increasing news coverage and the like, or to reduce its income by for instance offering advertisers bigger discounts. At best, if such tactics work, the position of the richer papers is undermined at no benefit to the others (though readers and advertisers might do well out of it); at worst all that happens is a steady escalation of the losses of the loss-makers.

Moreover, any increase in profits' taxation produces a disincentive to reduce costs: why bother fighting to reduce staffing levels or resist wage claims when most of the resulting saving is going to benefit someone else – especially a rival? Better, from a newspaperman's point of view, to save the tax by spending the money: on making the paper more competitive. . . . Even if the money raised is used, not to give direct grants, but to subsidise newsprint, the situation isn't greatly improved. That can only be an encouragement to use more newsprint, and, as we will be seeing, Fleet Street's troubles stem mainly not from using too little newsprint, but from using too much.

Taxing revenue (advertising revenue, of course: the ethos of newspapers automatically assumes advertising is bad and circulation revenue good. Taxing circulation revenue smacks of 'taxes on knowledge') avoids the disincentive to cost reduction produced by taxes on profits. But its likely side-effects are equally damaging. The effect on recipients is likely to be the same as a tax on profits: the primary effect on the payers of the tax however is likely to be an attempt to increase advertising revenue. If that were to be achieved by an increase in advertising rates, the effect might not be so bad. But that is a very scary thought to Fleet Street executives: much more likely is an increased attempt to improve sales volume through putting even more effort into improving the paper's attractiveness to advertisers (by increasing circulation, at least within the target market segment). And in a situation where the already successful are being driven to make themselves even more successful, the only result is likely to be a widening of the gap between the successes and the failures – the beginning of a spiral to destruction.

The second of the two longer-lived proposals for solving Fleet Street's economic problems while avoiding monopoly is simply that the State should provide printing facilities for newspapers in much the same way as the IBA (Independent Broadcasting Authority) provides broadcasting facilities to the independent television companies. That has several things against it. To begin with, if the concept of separate printing and publishing operations was valid in the newspaper industry, one could have expected that it would have evolved in the private enterprise situation, as it has with magazines and book publishing. In fact, the only national newspapers that do not control their own production (*The Guardian*, *The Observer*) are both hardly good advertisements for it – from the commercial point of view. It is difficult too to see how a satisfactory price level could ever be arrived at: or how anyone could decide which newspapers ought to be entitled to the service. The two things go together, since one solution could be to ration the service by price – offer it to the highest bidders. But that is hardly what the sponsors of the idea had in mind (though from a classical liberal-economic point of view it might be the best solution). If charges were to be set on a cost-plus basis, then it is difficult to see that anything would change at all, unless the production cost structure were to change considerably, which seems a rather rosy hope. And if charges were set below cost, thereby subsidising the publishing side of the industry, there is no way the service could be allocated without in effect introducing censorship (which, at least in this book, is considered undesirable). That after all has in practice been the fate of the IBA system.

There are other objections, notably from journalists who tend to see close integration between editorial and production as essential to proper news coverage. But the most interesting aspect of the opposition to the proposal was the steadfast way in which it was opposed by the unions – who might, in general, have been expected to welcome partial nationalisation on political grounds. On reflection however, their opposition is not surprising, on three grounds.

One is that, whatever the other flaws in the idea, it would make possible considerable rationalisations in the production system. Another is that the management of a nationalised printing corporation, under some governments at least, would not be anywhere near so susceptible to union pressure as the present publisher/printers. And the third is that the unions in general have no great incentive to seek or welcome any change in the set-up of the industry since they

B

are doing rather well out of the present situation. Which, if one pauses for a moment, casts a little doubt on the general assumption that the sorry profit records of the newspapers indicate that the industry is sick. Most of the companies may be: but it doesn't follow that the *industry* is. Print workers and journalists are not merely among the highest paid in Britain: as we will be seeing in Chapter 5, they lead the way, apart from some small groups of specialists. And there can be no doubt that Fleet Street's unskilled workers do better than any other unskilled group in the country.

Taken as a whole, therefore, the industry isn't doing too badly. The trouble the companies have is simply that not much of the value added ends up on the right side, for them, of the profit and loss account. Nevertheless there does remain some danger that the goose which lays the unions' golden eggs may well die on them, even if not (deliberately) at their hand. In the next few chapters we will be looking at some of the reasons why. But, in order to do that, there are some unusual features of the economics of newspapers, compared to other industries, that need to be briefly explained.

First of all, newspapers, unlike most industries, serve two markets simultaneously. By and large, something like half of the industry's income comes from the advertisers whose messages it carries. Half comes from the readers who buy it. It is a familiar point perhaps, and not worth dwelling on. But it is worth anticipating an argument I will be expanding later by pointing out now that the traditional view that newspapers (at least British national newspapers) are much cheaper to the reader than they would be if they carried no advertising is pretty wide of the mark. It's less true than is generally claimed for all newspapers, and for some the truth is the other way round. The reader subsidises the advertiser.

There is a similar, and not unrelated, division on the costs side. Apart from pure overheads, every newspaper (or magazine or book, for that matter) has two categories of direct cost, which roughly speaking come out about equal in size over the whole industry. The first category is commonly called 'first-copy' costs: i.e., the costs of editorial material, composing, plate-making and so on. The second category is called 'run-on' costs: the cost of actually printing ('machining') the copies and distributing them. 'First-copy' costs are therefore directly related to the number and size of the pages in the newspaper. 'Run-on' costs are related to both the number and size of pages and the number of copies printed. Increasing circulation therefore increases run-on costs but leaves first-copy costs unchanged: the situation that most mass-manufacturers find themselves in. Newspapers' unusual dual-market situation however leaves them caught in another way: increasing advertising sales increases the number of pages per issue, and therefore increases *both* first-copy and run-on costs.

There are a few key differences which need to be noted between the two markets and their related variable costs. Circulation is to all intents and purposes infinitely variable: but the number of pages can only increase or decrease in a small number of steps, each of substantial relative size. Essentially, tabloids can only change their pagination in multiples of four, while broadsheets can change (with some difficulty) in multiples of two. That is, the minimum change in pagination is normally something like 6 to 12 per cent of the paper's total size.

Within limits, therefore, direct run-on costs are virtually proportional to sales. First-copy costs don't however behave in that convenient way: their relationship to advertising sales is a step function. Squeezing more advertising into the same number of pages (at the expense of editorial coverage) incurs no extra cost at all. One might assume indeed that, since advertising plates are usually supplied by the advertiser, increasing the amount of advertising might actually save on composition costs. But in practice, as I'll be discussing later, print workers are paid for advertising matter 'as if' they had composed it themselves, so it makes no difference. However, crossing the advertising sales threshold that makes another two or four pages necessary is a very different matter. Even if the marginal cost of the extra pages is no higher than average (that is, if the extra pages cost no more to produce than the existing ones) the increase in costs due to the marginal advertisement is higher than the marginal revenue. In a situation, say, where a tabloid newspaper with 32 pages of which 14 are advertising goes to 36 pages to accommodate another page of advertising, the increase in revenue is only $1/14 = 7\cdot14$ per cent, while the increase in costs would be $4/32 = 12\cdot5$ per cent.

And the reality is worse than that. For while newsprint and distribution costs are fairly closely proportional to the number of pages (i.e. marginal costs equal the average), labour costs are not. The extra labour costs needed to produce the extra output are often horrendous, especially where the newspaper is breaking precedent by producing an abnormal number of pages. Thus, in the early spring of 1973, the managing director of the IPC newspapers announced with pride that the *Daily Mirror* (fighting back against *The Sun*'s attack) had for the first time in its history started regularly producing 40-page newspapers. He also announced, equally proudly, that in the first month there had been a record advertising revenue. He failed to point out (at least in the source I am quoting, *IPC News*) that in view of the exorbitant union demands IPC had agreed to in order to make the 40-page papers possible, even a record advertising revenue was not going to be enough to overhaul his record costs.

From an economic point of view, therefore, the volume of advertising is a much more important parameter than the volume of sales in determining costs. Selling more advertising may well be disastrous, whereas selling more copies is unlikely to do any serious harm.

Fleet Street in general recognises the distinction by offering its advertising managers greater rewards and respect than its circulation managers, and (with occasional exceptions, like *The Sun* at one time) by concentrating much harder on selling advertising than on increasing circulation. It seems reasonable therefore to start a more detailed look at the economics of the situation with a consideration of advertising in the next chapter. Chapter 3 then looks at circulation problems and Chapter 4 provides a case study to exemplify both, before I move on to tackle the subject of Fleet Street labour relations, which, while they are tangled and complex, have at least the merit of frequently being humorous in a sick kind of way.

2
Advertising

As I mentioned, the seriousness with which advertising is taken in Fleet Street is perhaps best shown by the respect with which those responsible for getting it are treated. Virtually universally, the job of advertising director carries with it a seat on the main board, while the responsibility for circulation very rarely gets that recognition. Moreover, the advertising department is the commonest general road to further promotion: leaving out the papers where the job is an 'in-family' perk, the majority of chief executives are ex-advertising men. Advertising managers and directors have bigger salaries than their circulation equivalents, as well as bigger offices, bigger expense accounts and bigger budgets (but not, normally, bigger staffs).

Commercially speaking there is no doubt about which of its two markets Fleet Street considers the most important. Even its attitude to market research is illuminative. Most papers pay a considerable amount of attention to reader research. IPC and Thomsons, notably, have sizeable and highly competent departments devoted to the subject (even though the sacking by Thomsons of Harry Henry a few years ago demonstrated the fate that awaits marketing men who are felt to be becoming too powerful). Depth and elaboration vary from company to company, but every newspaper management can fairly speedily lay its hands on a breakdown of its readership in terms of social and economic class, buying habits, age, and so on. But that information isn't used to increase circulation. It isn't used in the way, say, that Cadbury's might carry out market research in order to boost chocolate sales through new products or new packaging. Instead, the information is used by the advertising departments to plan their campaigns for selling the newspaper to advertisers and advertising agencies. Which accounts, to a great extent, for the elaboration of the research: it fits in with the way advertisers make their decisions.

Newspapers are therefore usually in the ironic position of knowing more about the way their readers live their lives and spend their money than they do about their tastes in newspapers – newspaper marketing departments are on the whole more use to the rest of industry than they are to their own circulation departments. But circulation problems are the subject of the next chapter. For the moment our concern is with the emphasis placed on the drive to sell advertising. And that is precisely what it is: a drive to *sell advertising*. For in Fleet Street the order of priority is, first, the volume of advertising sold; second, the revenue gained from it; and third, if at all, the profitability of it.

For people coming into the industry from outside it is a little difficult to believe (almost as difficult as the facts about the production situation which I'll be describing later), but the general run of Fleet Street advertising managers are never happier than when they are in a position to turn away advertising: in the way that, for instance, *The People* was in the late 'sixties. It becomes a reason for boasting and feeling superior to members of less fortunate departments on other newspapers. It even becomes a reason for delivering rose-coloured reports to senior management and shareholders. In general, it has the same result as a full order book on a shipbuilder or a machine-tool manufacturer. But with less justification. Unless he is daft enough to be quoting prices based on current costs, the ship-builder filling up a long order book is ensuring his future profits. The newspaper turning away advertising is only losing money.

Perhaps a close approximation to what the advertising manager considers heaven is the situation that British Leyland got itself into with the XJ series of Jaguars: demand wildly exceeding supply. But on the one hand, an order now for a Jaguar can be filled some time in the future: very rarely can that be done by newspapers. And on the other, at least British Leyland had the grace to be unhappy about the situation, even if they didn't do much about it except, crazily enough, take legal action to try and keep the secondhand price below the new.

For, difficult enough though it is to convince anyone in Fleet Street of it, the truth is that any situation in which demand is outstripping supply has got to signify one thing: the price is too low. It has to be a bad situation for the supplier unless he increases his prices. The only solution to the problem of the long queue is to shorten it by raising prices until enough people drop out to reassure you that you are in balance. But it isn't a solution Fleet Street has ever adopted: mainly because a long queue isn't even recognised as a problem.

Actually, it may seem a little odd to be talking about the problem of queuing advertisers, at least since the end of newsprint rationing in 1955. For the general impression that the industry gives is that it suffers from a chronic shortage of advertising, which varies only from the very bad, in recession periods, to the bearable, in boom times. The great wave of concern over the viability of newspapers in the early 'sixties (as well as the current one) had as its major theme the over-dependence of newspapers on advertising, with, as a necessary corollary, the assumption that there wasn't enough of it to go around. And, at least in popular mythology, the introduction of commercial television in 1955 is usually held to be the major reason for the shortage. But that is not an impression which is borne out by the facts. Undoubtedly the arrival of television had an initial impact, but since, say, 1961 the relative shares of the advertising market held by TV and national newspapers have remained remarkably constant, in money terms, at about 25 per cent and 18 per cent respectively. In their respective shares of advertising budgets, TV and national newspapers have therefore tended to come out about even. In terms of volume, however, there is much more to it than that. For over the twelve years, 1961–73, TV advertising rates just about kept pace with inflation, or moved slightly ahead of it. Newspaper rates on the other hand lagged way behind, increasing by less than 40 per cent over the period. Their constant share of revenue therefore has only been achieved at the expense of a considerable increase in volume.

At an international advertising conference in Vienna in 1973, some of these points were made, indirectly, by Frank Rogers, then the director of the Newspaper Publishers' Association. In what was at heart an attempt to demonstrate the superior cost effectiveness of newspapers as an advertising medium, he pointed out that in the years 1966–72, TV rates in the UK had risen by 80 per cent (twice the rise in retail prices) while newspaper rates had gone up by only 20 per cent. In the hands of someone selling advertising it sounds like a bull point for newspapers, and of course it is. Newspapers have become a much more cost-effective advertising medium than television. But as a comment on the management of newspapers, it is more of a criticism than a flattery. In television, all costs are effectively overhead: at least, none is directly related to the volume of advertising sales. Newspapers are not in that odd position: as in most industries, most of their costs are direct. And, as I pointed out earlier, those costs are much more affected by changes in advertising volume than they are by changes in circulation. The last thing that anyone in this position can afford to be caught up in is a price-cutting operation. Where marginal cost is higher than average cost, price-cutting is more like throat-cutting. Yet a price war is precisely what newspapers have been conducting against television and among themselves.

On the figures above, from 1966–72, newspapers halved their prices in constant money terms, while television prices doubled. In a nice justification of classical economics, the result was a massive increase in newspaper advertising, while the amount of television advertising stayed little more than constant (total television advertising time is of course subject to statutory control anyway). But of itself that contributed nothing to increasing television costs, while the rise in newspaper advertising guaranteed a massive increase in costs, irrespective of changes in wages and raw material prices.

The point can be made perhaps even more clearly over the period 1961–73: the period between the end of television's initial impact and the recent vast rise in newsprint costs, and therefore in some ways a period of relative stability. Taking 1961 levels as 100, by 1973 advertising rates had risen to 142 and advertising revenue to 194. Advertising volume had presumably therefore increased to around 136. There is admittedly a problem in that figures for volume of advertising are hard to come by. Advertising rates are published and advertising revenue too: but dividing one by the other to get 136 only produces a theoretical figure since no one keeps statistics on how much is actually charged for advertising – how much, that is, advertising salesmen are giving their customers in the way of dis-counts.

This practice of 'rate-busting' is sneered at and looked down on, but it is nevertheless common. Pre-Murdoch, the *News of the World* in particular had a reputation for it among the other popular Sundays, but the whole subject is impossible to investigate accurately. What is certain is that there was no counter-balancing over-charging. The estimate of a 36 per cent rise is therefore necessarily conservative.

It is true that over the period newspapers benefited from relative stability in newsprint prices. Over the twelve years, the price of news-print rose by only 20 per cent, and indeed dipped for a while in the middle. The other major component of direct costs however, labour, zoomed upwards, with wages rising by about 180 per cent.

Obviously, to contain the situation, the newspapers needed another source of extra revenue, and that was found from circulation sales. Between 1961 and 1973 cover prices rose on average by 140 per cent (neatly changing a threepenny paper in old coinage into three new pence) while sales volume slipped by only 9 per cent, generating a 130 per cent increase in sales revenue.

To clarify the position, the 1973 situation (with 1961 = 100) looked like:

Advertising rate	142	
Advertising volume	136	
Advertising revenue		194
Cover price	240	
Sales of copies	91	
Circulation revenue		230
Labour costs		280
Newsprint prices	120	
Newsprint consumption	133	
Newsprint costs		160

The conclusions are obvious. The industry spent the whole of the 'sixties engaged in a price-cutting war with television (except that television didn't fight back) not by actually cutting rates but by allowing them to fall behind inflation. As a result they achieved an increase in advertising revenue barely sufficient to cover the increase in direct costs attributable to it. They were only able to do this (and stay alive) for two reasons: because cover prices were pushed up quickly enough almost to cover increasing labour costs; and because the price of newsprint fell in constant price terms. Up till the 'seventies, the strategy had therefore 'worked'. The doom foreseen for the industry by many people in the early 'sixties hadn't arrived. Two national dailies, *The Times* and *The Sun*, had changed hands, but only one, the *Daily Sketch*, had actually folded. On average, the industry was roughly speaking about as well-placed at the end of the period as it had been at the beginning.

But its neck was now well and truly stuck out. The whole industry had become much more vulnerable to two things: any action that would prevent them continuing to put up cover prices in order to contain wage increases; and an end to the period of stable newsprint prices. Both things happened. On the cover price front the situation was perhaps not so bad as it might have been, The industry found itself theoretically subject to anti-inflation price controls, but by and large managed to argue its case for the increases it continued to want. On the newsprint front however it faced disaster: a doubling of prices in only a little over a year. The old strategy was no longer viable.

It is difficult to see how anyone could ever have thought it would be viable for long. A policy that depended on continuing stability of raw material prices in a world where every other commodity price was steadily rising (even now, the rise in newsprint prices over the last 20 years is only on a par with general inflation) ought to have looked suicidal from the start. If anyone had stopped long enough to think about it objectively, it would have been readily apparent. But no one did. And it's interesting to consider why they didn't.

At the time of the 1962 Royal Commission, and for many years afterwards, one of those truths that everybody knows (like 'the earth is flat') was that 'newspapers are too dependent on advertising'. Apart from any objective considerations, the slogan had a great deal of emotional support going for it. The ogre of advertisers' control over editorial matter didn't only arouse the battling instincts of every true-blooded journalist and left-wing politician. It also sounded pretty good to the public at large, and in particular to the kind of public-spirited people that get appointed to Royal Commissions. It even had some objective sense. For advertising revenue is highly cyclical whereas circulation revenue is singularly unaffected by the state of the economy. Ideally therefore the publishing industry ought to rely for its bread-and-butter income on its circulation, and take its jam, in the good times, from advertising. So from a sound corporate planning point of view, the assertion made sense.

What really went wrong was the way the maxim was transformed into action. It was translated to mean: 'We should therefore increase the proportion of circulation revenue to advertising revenue.' And that in its turn was developed into: 'We should increase cover prices', with the corollary 'and leave advertising rates as they are'.

There was nothing wrong with increasing cover prices, as the table above bears out: a 9 per cent drop in sales as the result of a 140 per cent increase in price isn't bad. In fact it indicates that cover prices were already too low, as the unions had been pointing out to the proprietors for some years.

But the rest was factually ridiculous. It appealed very much however to the advertising departments of the newspapers since it saved them any of the headaches involved in selling on any basis other than 'look how cheap we are'. It also appealed to managements generally because of something that is inevitably going to be a recurring theme of this book: their timidity, and in particular their timidity in face of the advertiser. Uniformly over the years the national newspapers have met the advertisers on self-conscious terms of inferiority. The advertiser is someone brighter, more powerful, more cunning, and generally someone not to offend. Certainly the newspaper manager is more afraid of the advertiser than the reader: the strategy of stinging the latter to avoid frightening away the former was therefore eagerly seized upon. So eagerly that the basic truth implied in that slogan 'newspapers are too dependent on the advertiser' was either overlooked or ignored. For if the slogan means anything, it must mean 'newspapers need too much advertising', not 'newspapers have too much advertising revenue'. And the policy of restricting rate rises could only have one effect: to worsen the dependence. For it ensured an *increased* need for advertising volume.

It isn't all that difficult to see. Assume a company that has initially sales revenue per issue of £200,000 and the same in advertising revenue. Overhead costs are, say, £100,000 and direct costs £250,000, so the profit per issue is a comfortable £50,000. Then assume the cover price is doubled, with no loss in circulation: sales revenue is now £400,000. Assume too that over the same period overhead and direct costs rise by only 80 per cent, much less, proportionately, than the cover price increase. Costs are now £630,000. If advertising revenue stays the same, the paper is now making a loss. If the advertising rate stays the same, then the paper is more dependent than before on increasing advertising volume. To restore its previous profit position it needs a 40 per cent increase in volume – except that that is likely to mean a 40 per cent increase in direct costs. The paper is in a bind it can't get out of.

It is in such a bind of its own making that Fleet Street now finds itself – made even worse by the fact that the only way it knows to increase advertising volume is by internecine battling on a price basis, and by the fact that for many papers the marginal costs of advertising are now above marginal income. Increasing advertising therefore only increases the losses.

The only paper actually to admit this (at the time of writing) is the *Daily Mirror*, whose advertising director announced to an internal conference of advertising staff in May 1974 that it now cost £514 to produce a column of advertising in the *Mirror*, while the net return from it was only £475. That, incidentally, appears to be average cost.

Marginal costs are much higher than average with the amount of bribery that has to be paid to the unions to produce extra pages. But marginal costs are not something that most people in the industry can bear to look at.

The same director also announced to the, presumably startled, gathering that this marked a reversal in the traditional economics of newspapers. No longer was the advertiser subsidising the reader: now the reader was subsidising the advertiser. Basically, he was right to say so. But he was wrong to imply that this was something new.

That newspapers are cheap to the reader because they are subsidised is another of those assertions that are invariably taken for granted, not only by the public at large but within the industry itself. Even in the last year or two it has been steadily promulgated by people who ought really to know better (for instance, *The Times*). Generally, it takes the form of asserting that if paper X didn't carry any advertising it would cost two, three or even four times as much. The calculation that produces those figures is based on assuming that, without advertising, the same amount of revenue would have to be dug out of the reader alone.

Thus a typical quality paper with say two-thirds of its revenue coming from advertisements would, the argument goes, have to cost 18 pence instead of 6 pence. A popular paper with maybe 40 per cent of its revenue from advertising would have to go up from 4 pence to 7 pence. And so on. But it is patently an inaccurate comparison. Effectively, the cost of producing say, a 32-page edition with 14 pages of advertising is being compared with the cost of producing a 32-page edition with no advertising. And that is really not the point: the comparison should be between a 32-page edition with 14 pages of advertising, and an 18-page paper. Then the situation looks very different. Assume the cover price is 4 pence and the advertising revenue per copy 2·67 pence – the 40 per cent case. Assume too that the newspaper is just breaking even, with its total costs working out at 6·67 pence per copy. If all costs were direct, the 18-page no-advertising paper would cost only $9/16 \times 6·67 = 3·75$ pence. Since the income would still be 4 pence, the paper would actually move from breakeven to profit. There would not need to be any price increase at all.

Assuming all costs are direct is admittedly pretty extreme. In fact, about 50 per cent of costs are normally directly proportional to paging: newsprint, ink, and distribution. A large proportion of wage costs, while not direct in a pure sense, also vary considerably with pagination: notably the bonuses that have to be paid for 'extra working'. Nearly everybody on the production side has to be paid extra for working on bigger papers, whether or not they actually do any work. It's not unreasonable to assume therefore that another 25 per cent of costs are direct in this sense. 25 per cent of the costs are therefore left to be treated as overheads.

In the case we've assumed, that means 1·67 pence represent fixed costs and 5 pence variable. The cost of the no-advertising issue then works out at $1·67 + 9/16 \times 5 = 4·5$ pence. By the time one allows for the saving in overheads due to not having to bother with advertising at all, the paper might well end up costing the same.

In any case, one doesn't have to go that far to argue that the traditional view of the subsidy is highly misleading and has been so for a long time. The criterion isn't necessarily that advertising rates are less than cost, or that the paper would be cheaper without advertising. The true criterion ought to relate the ratio of advertising to editorial space with the ratio of advertising to circulation revenue. In a completely 'fair' situation, the ratios ought to be equal. If the first is higher than the second then arguably the reader is subsidising the advertiser: only if the second is higher than the first is the reader getting his paper cheap. On that basis the reader started subsidising the advertiser on many papers some while ago. Even on the quality papers the advertisers pay much less of a subsidy than is generally recognised.

Accurate per-title figures are not easy to come by. But the readers of the *Mirror* and the then *Sketch* were subsidising the advertisers as long ago as 1958. Over the whole industry in 1961, the key ratio was 1·42: advertisers were subsidising readers by, say, 42 per cent. By 1972 the ratio was down to 1·17, with all the popular papers below that, and all the quality papers above it (though well down on ten years before). Since then the situation has got steadily worse, with cover price increases still keeping way ahead of the minimal increases in advertising rates that have taken place.

The fairest version of the subsidy assertion would therefore seem to be that over the popular press as a whole the cost of advertising is subsidised out of revenue from readers, while in the quality press a slightly larger subsidy is paid by the advertiser to the reader. (And that doesn't reflect a tougher attitude on the part of the quality papers to the big advertisers. The difference is accounted for by the much greater proportion of classified advertising carried by the quality papers. The instinctive fear of advertising rate increases doesn't apply anything like as much to small advertisements: the quality papers can therefore use the small advertisers to subsidise the big ones.)

As is obvious from the *Mirror* situation, this imbalance is beginning to be recognised in the industry. Not much is being done about it however, partly because of anti-inflation legislation, but more importantly because the instant response of any advertising manager to whom one suggests a rate increase is to assert that his customers wouldn't pay it. Of itself, in the 100 per cent way it is usually asserted, this is patently ridiculous. No market has perfect elasticity: especially if the rise is a joint one imposed by all suppliers.

It ought to be remembered too that advertising agencies, who have some say in their clients' decisions, would stand to gain even more by an increase in advertising rates than would the newspapers.

One would, of course, have to concede that a price increase would result in a fall in advertising volume. But the point that should have been emerging over the last few pages is that that is exactly what is needed. Fleet Street doesn't suffer from a shortage of advertising: it suffers, desperately, from trying to carry far too much. To get it back to health it needs, perhaps more than anything else, much less advertising at a much higher price.

If that is true of individual papers, it is even truer of the industry as a whole. In the years of the price war, the weaker papers have suffered more than the stronger as their advertisers have been wooed away by loss-leading rivals. Putting the situation into reverse, in a situation where the stronger papers are deliberately trying to reduce excess demand through higher prices, means that advertisers unwilling to pay the higher total charges would have to turn to the papers which are at present weaker. A lessening of the size of the cake (in volume terms) would mean a more equitable sharing of it.

Something like that situation existed, oddly enough, not very long ago, in the days of newsprint rationing. Then, advertisers who couldn't get into the stronger papers had to turn to the weaker ones, producing the rosiest period of prosperity for newspapers in decades. Currently, the world is again facing a newsprint shortage – treated properly, as an excuse for the reintroduction of (voluntary) rationing, that apparent threat could help to reproduce the golden days that ended in 1955.

But instead, Fleet Street sees it, as it sees most things, as a harbinger of doom. And if resistance to the whole idea of co-operating to restore advertising rates to something like the level of, say, 1948, remains solid, a harbinger of doom is just what it is likely to be.

3
Circulation

Pick a sales manager from any industry at random, and ask him what his sales were last month. He'll tell you: so many thousands or millions of pounds, dollars, yen or whatever currency he thinks in. Take a Fleet Street circulation manager and ask him the same question, and he'll tell you: so many million. Not pounds or pence, but copies. And for that matter, not total copies but copies per day. Of course any other industry will also quote you volume figures if you ask for them. And equally the circulation manager is capable of multiplying his circulation by the cover price and taking away the retail discount to give you a money figure, if you ask him specially. But it isn't money he thinks in. It may seem a trivial point. But in fact it is of critical importance.

Underlying this concentration on number of copies there are two basic factors. One is straightforwardly emotional. The other is a rationalisation of that emotion which will be presented by those who want to appear hard-headed.

The emotional one is simply that Fleet Street tends to reckon success in parochial terms. Points in the Fleet Street game are scored by selling more copies than one's rivals. Owners of newspapers with high and, better still, rising circulations feel happy and pat the heads of their editorial and circulation staffs: in their turn they feel secure and superior. In contrast, low and dropping circulations send shivers up the spine. There is one ground on which such an attitude is entirely expectable and sound. If the point of a newspaper is, à la Beaverbrook, to exert political, economic or social influence, then the more copies you sell the better. If the point of a newspaper is to make profits however, or even if the point is only to be self-sustaining, then the attitude is potentially disastrous. (High and low are of course comparative terms. *The Times* does not consider itself to be doing badly simply because it sells less than *The Sun*. The economic rationalisation for this we will be coming back to later. Emotionally however the low-circulation quality papers bolster their egos with the belief that the reason for their small sales is that they appeal to an intellectually and socially superior élite.)

The economic rationalisation of the attitude is simple enough. It is that the number of copies you sell determines the amount of advertising you get. The more readers you offer the advertiser, the more advertising he is going to place with you. On this count, the satisfaction of the quality papers with their low circulations is accounted for by the fact that they are serving an élite which is economically as well as socially superior. They are therefore of special interest to the advertiser. As a rule of thumb, that is reasonably true. But to make it the rationale for attempting to maximise circulation (within the socio-economic group being aimed at) makes a series of assumptions. They aren't normally made explicit. Once they are, the argument doesn't look so sound.

In the first place, from the point of view of the sociology of the industry, concentration on the number of copies sold underlines the relative positions of advertising and circulation in the hierarchy of esteem.

You sell copies in order to get advertising. You don't get advertising in order to sell copies (though some magazines do.) Circulation is secondary to advertising and you count the number of copies not the money you get for them. This relies of course on the perpetuation of the myth that the advertiser subsidises the reader: that advertising is inherently more profitable than circulation. Furthermore, it relies on the assumption that the value of the extra advertising will be worth, not only the cost of the extra pages, which, as we have seen, is doubtful, but also the cost of the extra circulation. (That's a charitable assertion: frequently the cost of the extra circulation is ignored.)

Effectively, the sequence involved is something like this: The paper puts on, say, an extra 10 per cent circulation. The editor or the circulation manager (usually the former) takes the credit, but both feel pleased. So does senior management. As a result, let's say, the paper takes on 10 per cent extra advertising. The advertising director feels pleased, though he may not be able to take all the credit. Revenue goes up 10 per cent irrespective of the split between circulation and advertising revenue. But (even assuming that marginal costs are equal to the average costs) the result is that the number of pages goes up 10 per cent and the number of copies also goes up 10 per cent. First-copy costs therefore go up by 10 per cent in line with revenue. Run-on costs however go up by over 20 per cent, and whatever the split between first copy and run-on costs, total variable costs have certainly gone up by more than the revenue has. In general therefore the paper has got less profitable.

There are various situations in which that could still mean an increase in profits. For instance:

—where the operation is already making large profits, they may still increase absolutely, even if return on turnover drops;
—where overhead costs (true overhead, not first-copy costs) are a substantial part of the total;
—where marginal costs are substantially below average costs;
—where the extra advertising can be squeezed into the same number of pages;
—where the advertising rate is increased.

All of these were at one time true in Fleet Street. The trouble is however that the assumption that they are valid has been carried on into a period where they aren't.

The first assumption, that the paper is already so profitable that its return on capital will go up even if its profit margin falls, is most distinctly no longer true in Fleet Street. No one in the industry consciously wants to see its margins go still lower, even where they are still positive.

The second assumption, that fixed overheads are still a major cost factor, has also become less and less true with every passing rise in wage rates and newsprint and distribution costs. All of these have gone up far faster than the cost of servicing capital, of paying rents, or rewarding senior management. Even if, as Fleet Street tends to do for reasons we will be coming to in later chapters, you take wage costs as fixed rather than variable (or variable upwards but not down), the critical rise that has triggered off the current crisis has been that in the price of newsprint, which by the time this book is being read is likely to have gone over 300 per cent from its level in January 1973. Countering a steep rise in raw material costs by using more raw materials is a strategy that one would not expect even Fleet Street to pursue. But it is where the logic of trying to increase circulation and advertising leads.

The third assumption, that marginal costs are below average costs, is one that isn't explicitly made in the industry. A generally hazy view that it can't cost much to print extra copies or add on a few extra pages suffices for most people. The facts of the matter are partly that the bribes which have to be paid to get workers to produce extra pages, or even to print and handle extra copies, heavily outweigh any benefit which spreading overhead costs over longer runs may bring, and partly that the cost-structure of the industry guarantees that such efforts are anyway self-defeating. An arithmetical argument may make the situation clearer. For simplicity's sake let us assume that the newspaper's cost structure consists of overheads ($\emptyset$), first-copy labour costs (I), run-on labour and distribution costs (R), and newsprint (N). Costs after a 10 per cent increase in circulation and advertising are then $\emptyset + 1 \cdot 21N + p^2R + pI$, where p is the multiplier on labour costs resulting from a 10 per cent increase in work. If p is also held to $1 \cdot 1$ (10 per cent), then the condition for an increase in profitability is:

$$(\emptyset + R + I + N)\, 1.1 > \emptyset + 1 \cdot 1I + 1 \cdot 21\,(R + N)$$
$$\text{which simplifies to } \emptyset > 1 \cdot 1\,(R + N).$$

That is, overhead costs must be more than 10 per cent greater than run-on costs. First-copy costs are irrelevant. There isn't a newspaper in Fleet Street genuinely in that position.

Of course the value of p is important. It is unlikely that the amount that will have to be paid in extra wages will correspond exactly to the amount of work involved. Usually in practice it will be much higher. But even if $p = 1$ (i.e., the extra work is done for *no* extra wages) the condition still remains $\emptyset + I + R > 1 \cdot 1N$. That is, newsprint costs must be less than 47·5 per cent of total costs.

That is a not unreasonable condition (though it may become less reasonable if the cost of newsprint continues to rise substantially). The linked condition that wages (not wage rates, but the total wage bill) must stay constant in spite of the increase in work is however untenable. For one thing, it would mean the abandonment of the piecework system that applies to most Fleet Street workers.

The last situation, where extra advertising can be carried in the same number of pages, is a more realistic one. It applies to *The Morning Star* for instance. It probably, to a limited extent, applies to several other papers. But for it to apply significantly it must be true that the newspaper is already carrying too many pages (by commercial criteria: the criticism can hardly be applied to a paper like *The Guardian* which has explicitly abandoned commercial criteria in determining pagination).

A simpler way of reducing costs would therefore be to reduce the existing number of pages. The argument against it will be that that would reduce circulation. Indeed the reason for the excess pages is likely to be that the newspaper is attempting to increase circulation. But that is evidently a vicious circle. We carry excess pages to increase circulation in the hope that the increased circulation will indirectly pay for the excess pages. The only thing that gives that argument sense is if increased circulation is seen as an end in itself.

The fourth situation is perhaps the most frequently presented as a rationalisation. It has something in it, in that an increase in circulation will usually lead to an increase in advertising rates. While advertising isn't officially sold on a 'per thousand' basis, it is usually valued that way by advertisers. Indeed, to increase circulation and pull in extra advertising *without* increasing advertising rates is not far from a classic recipe for disaster. For in that case revenue only increases proportionally with the circulation increase, while as the argument above shows, a significant part of costs rise with the square of the increase. Profitability unconditionally worsens. It does so even if overhead costs become a smaller proportion of total costs. The argument that 'we must sell more to cover our overheads' only applies if the extra sales improve profits: but that is a mistake which has been made in industries other than Fleet Street, notably in the package-tour business.

However, if we assume that rates increase in proportion to the improvement in circulation, the situation becomes more reasonable. But it is not so clearcut as tradition would indicate. To investigate it, it will be helpful to introduce a few definitions, the most important of which is the concept of 'advertising profitability' which we can define as advertising revenue less run-on costs. We can also now ignore overheads, since we will be concerned with changes in total profits, not the profit margin on sales.

If we make the same division of costs into first-copy and run-on, and we assume that circulation, advertising and the advertising rate all increase by the same fraction 'p', and further repeat the assumption that the extra newsprint costs the same per ton, and labour costs are proportional to the increase in work, then the criterion that an increase in circulation leads to an increase in profits is

$$C(1+k)-N(1+a) > C(p+p^2)-N(ap+p^2)$$

That inequality can be transformed into limits for the value of p, with the following rather complex results:

1. Where advertising profitability is zero, then an increase in circulation exaggerates the present position: i.e., profits are made larger but so are losses.
2. Where advertising profitability is greater than zero, an increase in circulation will increase profits *unless* the newspaper is currently loss-making, and the advertising profitability is less than the loss.
3. Where advertising profitability is less than zero, an increase in circulation will decrease profits *unless* the enterprise is currently profitable and the loss on advertising is less than the total profits.

Varying the simplifying assumptions about the proportionality of changes makes the algebra involved much more complex. But in general it is true that reliance on increasing circulation and advertising, even at higher rates, is unjustified if

1. Labour costs go up by more than the work involved (i.e., if overtime has to be paid).
2. The cost of extra newsprint is higher than the average cost.
3. Advertising rates go up by less than the circulation.

Each of those situations is rather more likely in current circumstances than their converse.

In sum, therefore, the hope that increasing circulation will help a newspaper in depressed circumstances is a pretty vain one. The hope that a loss situation can be turned into a profitable one by that road alone is an even emptier one. (There is only one exception: where by increasing its circulation one newspaper can drive another out of business, and establish a monopoly situation in its segment of the market. Even then, however, the increased profitability only comes about if the monopoly is used to increase cover prices or advertising rates, not directly through the circulation increase.)

If selling more copies is no remedy for distress, selling them at a higher price obviously may be. Over the last decade Fleet Street has indeed lost its earlier inhibitions about raising prices. Since the Royal Commission of 1962, cover prices have been raised by something over 300 per cent without causing any major contraction in sales volume.

Cover price increases alone have kept most Fleet Street papers healthy, although the addiction to increases has become such that some papers at least have become over-dependent on price increases for continuing existence. Even the *Daily Mirror*, viewed as unassailably profitable just a few years ago, by mid-1973 had become desperate for a one-penny price increase (15 years ago newspapers only cost the equivalent of one penny) to stay in the black. The refusal of the government to allow the increase in 1973 left the paper in fact with its first loss in decades for the year 1973/4.

By and large, as I pointed out in the last chapter, cover prices, unlike advertising rates, have more or less kept pace with percentage rises in costs. Absolutely, this hasn't meant enough increase in revenue to compensate for the increase in costs, but it has helped.

It is questionable, however, how much longer it can go on helping. One can't help feeling (though without any objective evidence) that there has to be a limit . . . there has to be a point at which cover price increases result in a reduction of sales and even revenue. If that reduction is accepted and leads as it should to compensating cost reductions, that might not be such a bad thing. Unfortunately it's more likely that it will lead to increased expenditure on first-copy costs – editorial, promotion campaigns, increased pagination, and so on – which will outweigh the savings in run-on costs.

Moreover, it is ironic that the newspapers only started to use cover price as an effective way of raising extra revenue at more or less the same time as successive governments started interfering with the price mechanism. I've already mentioned the unfortunate effect on *Daily Mirror* finances of having a rise delayed. Should any effective anti-inflation measures be introduced, it's not inconceivable that further cover price increases might be barred altogether. That would mean the newspapers being forced to take the cold turkey cure for their current addiction, and the process like all cold turkey cures could be extremely painful. Without price increases as a useful narcotic, maintaining health is going to be a matter of increasing efficiency.

The fact that cover prices have been heavily increased while advertising rates have remained depressed is interesting, among other reasons, for the further illustration it gives of the relative status of the two areas. Circulation departments of Fleet Street were as opposed to cover price rises as their advertising colleagues were opposed to rate increases. But unlike their colleagues, they failed.

One reason of course is that senior management (indeed everyone on the staff) considers themselves as competent to judge the effects of a cover price rise as any circulation specialist. Another is that raising the cover price is essentially a simple decision, not like making complex changes to a rate card. A third is that advertising (display advertising at any rate) is sold to a relatively small number of people, and the advertising specialist can proffer his personal knowledge of how those people will react in support of his arguments, whereas the paper itself is sold to an amorphous mass of readers. And a fourth is that senior management is much more likely to include people with an advertising background and therefore sympathetic to the arguments of the advertising department. But the most potent reason is the lower esteem in which the circulation function is held. It is unthinkable that changes to the advertising rate should be made without the approval of the advertising manager. It is almost as unthinkable that anyone should ask the approval of the circulation department for a cover price increase.

To some extent there is an objective reason for the difference. On the whole, the functions of the advertising department correspond more or less to those of the sales department in an orthodox organisation. The circulation department, however, corresponds much more to what in most companies would be called the distribution function. The concern of circulation representatives and circulation managers is mainly with making sure that the wholesaler/retailer gets the copies he has ordered. Traditionally it has very little to do with inducing him to order more, though the circulation representative may be concerned with putting up the posters that are the industry's only flirtation with point-of-sale display.

In addition to the circulation department so-called, and usually operating independently of it, there is likely also to be a promotion department, carrying out the functions of an advertising department in normal industry, as well as being responsible for organising special campaigns and stunts, like competitions and the sponsorship of sports events (a field in which newspapers pioneered, though they have recently been overtaken by other industries, notably the tobacco manufacturers).

Usually a great deal of creativity and imagination goes into the work of the promotion department, and some of the campaigns ('Lobby Lud') have stayed in the memory long after the newspapers that employed them have vanished. Unfortunately, the promotion department is effectively decoupled from concern with the price level, as well as from the profitability of the increased sale. Their essential brief is, given the price level, to sell more copies, and viewed with that much simplicity they on the whole do quite well. It isn't their fault if their activity only increases the troubles of the newspaper. In the short term at least, that is all that they can do. For as I have demonstrated, increases in circulation unaccompanied by increases in advertising rates only decrease profits, given the cost and revenue structure of the industry.

For a circulation increase to lead to an increase in advertising rates (and therefore make an improvement in profitability possible, though not certain), it has to remain established for some while. And while promotions and advertising can attract purchasers they can do nothing to make them stay with the paper. The only thing that can do that is the editorial content.

Now if the newspaper is viewed as a non-commercial enterprise, the editorial department can have many roles. But if the assumption is made that at least part of the objectives of a newspaper is to make profit, then the role of the editorial department within that must be to attract and keep the loyalty of readers – the right kind of readers, if the newspaper has a deliberate policy of market segmentation. Nobody else can do it. The critical role that editorial plays in building and maintaining circulation is universally recognised in Fleet Street, to the extent that the most exposed person in a situation of declining circulation is usually the editor, assuming he cannot successfully get rid of the buck either downwards to his department heads or upwards to the board or the proprietor. Normally, he will be able to do this in cases where the titular 'editor' is evidently not the person ultimately responsible for editorial content.

But what isn't recognised usually is that the role of the editorial function in this regard is virtually identical with what in classical management theory is referred to as the marketing function. The kernel of marketing is matching the product to the market: the only people in Fleet Street who have any effect on that task are the editorial staff. Yet so far is the point missed that in some of the more 'advanced' groups (the Thomson organisation for example) attempts have even been made to graft a 'marketing department' on to the traditional organisation.

The only sensible place to fit such a unit into a newspaper organisation is under the editor: though even then it would be better to ensure that the people who hold down the senior editorial positions themselves command the relevant skills and knowledge to operate in a modern market-oriented manner. But that solution falls foul of the generally pernicious attempt to distinguish between the commercial and editorial functions of the newspaper, and to ensure that neither is contaminated by the other. So marketing units are installed in the chain of command that leads to the general manager or the managing director or whoever is held responsible for commercial affairs generally. They operate independently of the editorial function, which either misunderstands, misapplies or simply ignores them. And uniformly they fail. One lesson that can be drawn from the comparative records of *The Sun* and the *Mirror* is that, by and large, unless the marketing/editorial identification is understood, one is better off without a marketing department than with one.

Once it *is* understood, however, the logic that says that the editing of the newspaper, in the sense of the management of its content and appearance, should be closely linked organisationally with the present circulation and promotion departments is more apparent. So too is the converse that the traditional view of the editorial function links two essentially dissimilar roles: product design and production. There is no sensible reason other than tradition why the jobs usually classified as editorial should be closely linked, and separated off from other functions.

The line operations of a newspaper fall naturally into three groups: those concerned with building and maintaining advertising sales, those concerned with building and maintaining circulation, and those concerned with physical production. As in any other industry they interact, and need co-ordination if they are to operate together profitably. To assume that one can set out simply to maximise advertising revenue, maximise circulation revenue, and minimise production costs is, as I've demonstrated, one road to disaster. But the line organisation needs to fall along those lines if it is not to be distorted out of all touch with reality. And forcing on to the organisa-tion an arbitrary distinction between 'commercial' and 'editorial' activities, especially when the distinction is heightened by mutual disrespect and antagonism is one way of producing just that kind of distortion. It is likely to remain, however, since the division goes to the heart of the emotional attitudes of most people in the industry. That much prejudice is unlikely to be overcome by reason.

In particular, the identification of the editorial role with that of marketing in the classical management organisation is likely to raise protests from those whose overt concern is with the ethics of journalism. The identification smacks of denying the importance of those ethics. Yet in reality the opposite is true. To identify editorial with marketing is only to recognise where ethical considerations are most important. For it is precisely in the marketing function that ethical considerations (at least, customer-company ethics) become most important. It is the duty admittedly of the editorial function to maintain the quality of the service provided to the reader. But that same duty exists in other industries too, and in those that recognise it (which is probably most of them, *pace* Nader *et al.*), it is an essential part of product design and development, which, in a properly organised company at least, are themselves part of the marketing function.

In any case, if the present fragmented state of control over circulation levels, split between a low-level circulation department, a promotion department solely concerned with transient increases in copies sold, and an editorial department at heart unconcerned with 'commercial' matters, then there is unlikely to be any need for anyone to concern themselves with ethics.

So far, we have given detailed attention to the advertising and circulation sections of the newspaper's market and the way it approaches them. Production obviously has to follow. But before we move on to it, it is worth some time looking at an extended case study which encapsulates much of what I have been saying. Admittedly, it is to some extent an egregious study: the speed with which money was lost still remains some kind of record. But the attitudinal failings it reveals are symptomatic. It is the story of the *Mirror* Magazine.

4

Example – The *Mirror* Magazine

It may not have been the biggest single loss-making operation in Fleet Street history. But it was certainly the fastest. Launched in the autumn of 1969 (two weeks late thanks to labour disputes) the weekly colour supplement to the *Daily Mirror* (the *Mirror* Magazine) lasted a little over six months at a loss rate that approached a million pounds a month.

Its story is therefore exceptional. But even an extreme can serve an exemplary purpose. Especially since it supplies some instances of the kind of thinking and decision-making, and the attitudes that underlie them, which are typical of Fleet Street. In particular they are typical of what has happened whenever the industry has attempted to combine 'modern' methods with its traditional ones.

Colour supplements made their appearance in Britain in February 1962 with the launch of the *Sunday Times* colour magazine. After a very shaky start, complicated by a change of editorship shortly before the launch, the *Sunday Times* supplement established itself very quickly as a useful adjunct to the newspaper's advertising revenue, and even as a circulation-booster. *Sunday Times* and *Observer* circulations had both dropped in 1961 as a result of the arrival of the *Sunday Telegraph*, though the new paper hadn't had as much impact as its publishers had hoped. But the introduction of the colour supplement restored the *Sunday Times* position: it was therefore followed as soon as practically possible by *The Observer*.

The Telegraph group, eager to get its own share of the new vein of advertising that the colour supplements were mining, adopted a slightly different approach. Instead of appending a colour supplement to the *Sunday Telegraph* (the lowest-selling of the three quality Sundays, and anyway basing its advertising appeal on the fact that it was small and readable) one was tacked on to the Friday edition of the *Daily Telegraph*. All three quickly became part of the established Fleet Street scene. But through the mid-'sixties there were no further additions. Neither *The Times* nor *The Guardian* could easily have afforded the launch costs, and in any case *The Times* was shortly to be assimilated by the *Sunday Times*. And the readership of *The*

Financial Times, while admirably suited to many advertisers, had not enough particular appeal to the kinds of middle-class consumer advertisers that filled the colour supplements to overcome its small circulation.

And the economics of popular newspapers are signally different from those of the quality press.

The *Daily Mirror* in particular preferred to investigate other ways of introducing colour into newspapers. Indeed, the presses at the new *Mirror* building into which the paper moved at the beginning of the 'sixties were designed from the start for easy conversion to colour. Moreover, there was less incentive for the *Mirror* and the IPC Sundays to experiment with run-of-the-press colour than for the other populars. The only outlet for advertisers who wished to use colour for mass-appeal advertising at that time was the magazine industry. And IPC already controlled most of that. For the *Mirror* or *The People* to attempt to take a share of that market would be robbing Peter to pay Paul.

The *Mirror* management was therefore content to sit back and watch other papers, like the *Express*, lose fairly substantial amounts of money on prestigious, though unprofitable, occasional colour pages. For the long-term, they developed instead plans for the decentralisation of newspaper production. The principle here was that the development of facsimile transmission would make possible the local printing, on ten to twenty small plants, of a centrally produced (using computer composition) master edition. The local plants would be offset litho, and capable of producing in colour from the start. (Two of these plants were actually set up. The one in Belfast was dogged by labour troubles until it was finally bombed by the IRA. And the much larger one in Glasgow came into operation in 1973, though in its first year it lost £77,000 and it is used to produce *The Daily Record* – a separate paper from the parent in London.)

But by 1968, when development of this project was at its height, it was obviously going to be both a long-term and highly expensive project. And the imminence of ITV's shift to colour was making everyone highly sensitive to the need to provide colour facilities to advertisers. (Not necessarily to *editors*: but this point was lost sight of later.) Advertisers would prefer the colour of television to the black-and-white of newspapers – at least, so it was believed. Moreover, there was another possible defensive reason for the *Mirror* providing colour facilities in a hurry. While there was no thought as yet of his buying *The Sun*, Rupert Murdoch had recently acquired control of the *News of the World*, IPC's only significant rival, then, in the mass-circulation field. There was a strong feeling that he might well add a colour supplement to the paper, taking advertising away from IPC's mass circulation magazines. A pre-emptive launch by the *Mirror* of a colour supplement would remove that danger.

There were, of course, complicated problems. Notably, such a launch would still be likely to bleed away advertising from the popular magazines. The threats from ITV and Rupert Murdoch however lessened the significance of this danger. If Peter was to be robbed anyway, the money might as well be used to pay Paul. And one thing the project *would* do was create work for IPC's Printing Division, then desperate for increased throughput in its massive gravure plant at Watford.

When the newly formed Newspaper Division of IPC put forward its proposal for the launch, it therefore had the support and collaboration of the Printing Division. And the misgivings in some areas of the Magazine Division were stilled by the thought that Murdoch was being forestalled.

In any case, many of the people who were possible opponents of the idea were pre-empted when some of its advocates leaked to the industry newspaper *Campaign* that the *Mirror* was going to launch the Magazine. Subsequently the project was presented to a corporate staff group for analysis, but there was a certain abstract unreality about the situation. Going back on the announcement would have caused the corporation to lose face, in an industry which on the whole sets more store by face than profit.

The staff group reported in March 1969, with a recommendation that the Magazine go ahead. (There was a minority view, put forward by the then company secretary, that IPC couldn't afford the risks involved should it fail. But in the general atmosphere of euphoria, this was overridden.)

The recommendation was not however euphoric. It estimated that the Magazine, if everything went reasonably well, would just about break even, but it was swayed by the strategic arguments about the need to offer colour advertising to counter the effect of the arrival of colour TV. (After investigation, the threat of a colour supplement in the *News of the World* was ruled out.)

Moreover, there was a key reservation. The group was operating without any estimates of the price-elasticity of advertising demand.

An external advertising agency as well as the internal advertising department had produced estimates of total demand. But it was impossible to get either source to produce an estimate of how that demand might vary with price per page. The view with which the group had to try to cope was that the price-elasticity was, in effect, finite: at £x per page the revenue would be £y, and at anything higher than £x the advertising just wouldn't sell.

The group was forced to take its own view; it estimated that, at a colour advertising rate of £8,800 the Magazine could just do better than break even. The launch was given formal corporate approval.

It was planned for the middle of September, 1969. For the remaining five months of the financial year (to the end of February) it was estimated that the Magazine would carry 864 pages in 24 issues, 466 of them (54 per cent) advertising. Net advertising revenue was forecast at £3·1 million (£6,650 per page), and total costs at £2·9 million.

'Costs' here referred mainly to the charges made to the Newspaper Division by the Printing Division for printing the Magazine. These were based on the assumption that the increased throughput in the Odhams plant would allow improved utilisation of the plant, and the extra work would enable the plant's management to negotiate improved productivity with the unions. Given the *Mirror*'s circulation, the costs were estimated at £3,375 per page. Paper and ink came to £1,662 per page, distribution roughly £1,266, and 'fixed' costs (printing labour, editorial and advertising) £700 (on a 32-page issue).

Cracks began to show within a few weeks. In May, the Newspaper Division revised its forecasts for the 1969/70 corporate plan. The division's advertising department had now decided that advertising 'couldn't' be sold at the £8,800 rate. The rate was reduced to £7,750. At this figure the forecast was that £3·1 million revenue could still be earned, though at the cost of producing 968 pages, 508 of them advertising (52 per cent). The extra costs of doing so were reckoned at £3·2 million, producing a moderate loss of £0·1 million.

That seemed bearable, and the corporation pressed on. An editor was chosen, not unreasonably, from the *Mirror* staff. In line with then-current IPC organisational policy a publisher was also appointed to take overall responsibility. The man chosen was Dennis Hackett, who had previously achieved a great deal in the consumer Magazine Division, particularly as the editor of the magazine *Nova*, and was obviously highly talented.

Arguably, however, they were the wrong talents. The *Mirror* Magazine would have a guaranteed weekly sale, and though it would need to attract readers in order to attract advertisers, finding those readers was not going to be so critical a problem. In launching a normal, counter-sale publication there are sound reasons for choosing a publisher with editorial background and skills (viz., what I wrote about marketing in the last chapter). In this case however it could be little more than wasteful duplication: the critical skills were going to be commercial and financial, not editorial.

Moreover, going to the Magazine Division at all for a publisher revealed the existence of a critical misunderstanding. The *Mirror* Magazine was to look very much like a consumer magazine, but the resemblance would be only skin-deep, and while a talented cosmetician might be necessary, the proper place for him wouldn't be in the driving seat.

For the economics of a publication with a guaranteed distribution but no cover-price revenue are not those of a consumer magazine. They are the economics of a controlled circulation journal, of which IPC had many, most at least of them well-run, in another division, IPC Business Press. Generally, the business press division of IPC had been the best run of the subsidiaries, in the sense of being normally the most efficient and reliable in achieving its targets, even though it was not always the most profitable.

It is probable that a publisher from that division, with the right background in producing publications solely dependent on advertising revenue, might have seen the problems more clearly. He might too have had enough confidence in his judgement of commercial matters to make it stick against pressure from higher in the Newspaper Division, habituated as that had become to subsidising its advertisers from circulation revenue.

But that possibility was ignored. The Magazine went into detailed planning with no one with experience of similar ventures in its senior team.

Then the cracks began to widen. This time the problems arose in the Printing Division. Originally, that division's euphoric reception of the Magazine project had been due to the belief that it would enable the profitability of the Watford plant to be increased through heightened utilisation, and also that the presence of the extra work would allow the management to negotiate improved productivity with the unions.

It didn't work out that way. The project was received antagonistically by the unions, unanticipated extra labour had to be signed on to carry out the work, and negotiations were deadlocked to the point where the launch of the Magazine had to be delayed by a fortnight, to October 1, 1969. In spite of their increased costs, the charge that the Printing Division was to make to the Newspaper Division remained the same. Nevertheless the delayed launch meant that the newspaper division needed to recalculate its profit-and-loss figures. This was done in August, and the net result was a scaling down of anticipated revenue to £2·2 million gross, and £1·86 million net. Costs were also scaled down, but only marginally, to slightly under £3 million. After minor allowances for increased sales of the *Daily Mirror* and savings on *Daily Mirror* publicity, the Magazine was projected to lose £935,000 from launch to the end of the financial year.

The change was too much of course to be due only to a two-week delay in launching. No more changes had been made to advertising rates, but as the launch date grew closer severe adjustments had been made to sales forecasts. Over the five months the Magazine was now projected to get only 314 pages of advertising, a drop of 38 per cent from the previous estimate of 508. At the same time the total number of pages was only planned to go down by 27 per cent to 714. For the first time there were now expected to be more editorial than advertising pages.

In fact, there was now officially a 'quota' of advertising pages of 50 per cent. However, on issues where the expected amount of advertising was below quota, there were no plans to reduce pagination . . . merely to expand editorial.

With the Newspaper Division now projecting losses of nearly £1 million, the hopes of extra profitability in the Printing Division looked distinctly jaded; with the ever-present danger that Magazine advertising would be taken away from other group publications, and the disappearance of the threat of a *News of the World* colour magazine, another company – at least a company in another industry – might now have had second thoughts about going ahead. This was the last point at which the idea could have been dropped without incurring any great damage through laying off of staff.

Moreover, just at this particular point, IPC itself was going through a period of financial stress, to put it mildly. Corporate financial planning had only recently been introduced into the company, but it was beginning to produce results. The forecast compiled in August

1969 of the year's results showed profits (assuming £140,000 loss on the Magazine) of £11·3 million as against a planned £12·9 million. Earnings looked like being £6·3 million against the planned £7·3 million. But more serious problems still were evident from the cash-flow projections. In the six months up to and including August, the IPC divisions had been expected to remit £5·7 million in cash to the centre: they had in fact remitted £800,000. The corporation was evidently heading for serious cash problems that could only be made much worse by the escalating losses on the Magazine.

But in fact no serious consideration was given at this stage to killing the project. Most importantly perhaps, too much prestige was at stake. There had been vast amounts of publicity given to the Magazine, especially of course in the trade press. The idea of not going ahead would have been construed as cowardice: the industry's demands for bravura and machismo in its leading figures would not permit withdrawal at this stage.

Moreover, while corporate financial planning had started in the group, it is doubtful whether many people, especially in the Newspaper Division, were taking it seriously. The sheer fact that corporate planners were still working to an expected loss of £140,000 on the Magazine while divisional projections were showing £935,000 indicates fairly strongly the distinction being made between 'real-life' and the 'corporate plan'.

Inevitably the Magazine moved ahead to a well-publicised launch on October 1. In spite of the editorial bias in the management team, initial reader reactions to the Magazine were dismal. There were countless tales of *Mirror* buyers leaving the Magazine behind in the shop when they bought the newspaper. Later, the trade paper *Campaign* was to comment: 'When it appeared, agency reaction to the editorial was that IPC had fallen flat on its face. Views were varied, but largely anti. It was, they said, too pop, too up-market, too vulgar, too sexy. They didn't like the colour clash between ads and editorial – they didn't think it was like the *Mirror*.'

Objectively, the merit of the editorial content is impossible to assess. *Campaign*, when the Magazine eventually folded, devoted several pages to attempting the assessment, without demonstrating any conclusion. (It's worth remembering that the editorial content of the original *Sunday Times* colour supplement also met with a horrified response from most experts.)

Perhaps the most cogent point was that the National Readership

C

Survey eventually (February 1970) showed the Magazine's readership to be lower (at 29·3 per cent of all adults) than that of the *Mirror* itself (36·4 per cent). But in all likelihood none of the controversy over the editorial, fascinating though it may have been to people in the industry, had any effect at all on the success or failure of the Magazine. Nobody had to be induced to buy it. And while advertising sales are affected by the advertiser's concept of the number and kind of people who read a publication, the Magazine had a ten-week deadline. Reader reaction couldn't have had any effect on sales before Christmas 1969 and it is unlikely that it had any effect before the end of the first financial year.

And the situation was becoming desperate long before that.

By the early part of December, after some eight issues, the projected loss for both Newspaper and Printing divisions together had risen yet again to £1·4 million. The popular reason given was that the Magazine had failed to attract enough advertising. And indeed, in the first quarter its advertising revenue was estimated by the marketing department at £1,192,700 gross, instead of the last (August) forecast of £1,420,800. If costs had stayed as forecast, revenue failings would therefore have accounted for £228,100 of the missing £450,000.

But referring to that as a failure to 'attract advertising' masked a significant point. The August estimates, based on a card rate of £7,750 per colour page (and £4,500 in black and white), had assumed an average net income per advertising page of some £6,000. The actual rate achieved in the first quarter was only £5,114. The number of advertising pages sold was virtually on target: the *price* at which they had been sold had been, on average, 15 per cent off the card rate.

That had some interesting consequences which, while they were raised at the time, led to no action. According to the earlier projections in the range of pagination being utilised (between 24 and 40 pages), the Magazine cost some £3,375 per page to produce. The net amount being received per advertising page therefore covered the costs of approximately 1½ pages. The necessary implication was that at this price and this cost level, the Magazine would only break even if it were 66 per cent advertising.*

---

*However, in reality, printing charges, trade allowances and distribution costs at that time added up to £4,840 per page for a 24-page issue, £4,050 for 32, and £3,640 for a 56-page issue. That is, on a 40-page issue, one advertising page paid for something under half an editorial page: on a 24-page issue it paid for one seventeenth. A 40-page issue broke even with 10 pages of editorial and a 24-page issue with one page of editorial.

Yet the quota of advertising remained 50 per cent. Even if that quota had been filled, the losses would have been substantial: effectively advertising was being sold at below cost (just as it is in most popular papers today). The more advertising sold, therefore, the bigger the loss. The efforts to save the Magazine by selling more advertising were therefore suicidal (as General Dynamics found when they got into a similar mess with the Convair 880): and the diagnosis that the Magazine was in trouble because sales were too low was fundamentally in error.

By December, therefore, there was some feeling at corporate level that the Magazine ought to be discontinued. Unless, of course, either costs could be brought down or the advertising page rate pushed up. Neither looked a practical possibility: the first because of the state of labour relations in the Printing Division, and the second because of the unalterable and dogmatic position of the advertising specialists that no advertising could be sold at more than the going rate.

Feelings among the headquarters staff were however of little importance. Despite the introduction of formal control systems that were tighter than anything IPC had been used to in the past (on paper), in reality the centre had still failed to achieve any meaningful control over the activities of the Newspaper Division, with its status as the original heart of the corporation and the contributor of the biggest slice of income.

By January the situation had deteriorated further. The achieved rate per page had now dropped to £4,100. Once 508 pages of advertising had been expected to bring in £3·1 million. In August the forecast had dropped to 314 pages bringing in £2·2 million. Now, with three of the five months gone, 394 pages of advertising were expected, but the revenue from them had dropped to £1·6 million, emphasising further that the failure was not in selling advertising, but in getting a valid price for it.

As a result the expected loss in 1969/70 was now up to £1·7 million in the Newspaper Division, with, as far as anyone could tell, a further £500,000 loss in the Printing Division at the going transfer price. So a committee was appointed to investigate the question of closure.

The committee reported to the IPC Board in February. Its projections were really of unrelieved gloom. Its forecast of the 1969/70 loss in the Newspaper Division was £1·7 million. (Advertising pages were now expected to earn £5,500 net). For 1970/71 the loss was expected to be at least a million – a forecast that was moderately optimistic since it assumed a revenue of over £7 million in twelve months, as against the £1·6 million that had been earned in five. (If the achieved rate of revenue had been projected into the future, the 1970/71 loss would have come out at over £3 million. But this was a possibility the reporting committee preferred to ignore.)

The economics of the Magazine were not analysed in the report. Neither was the desirability of increasing page rates referred to. While the report talked of increasing revenue, it did so on the assumption that the page rate would be the same. Indeed the report spent a great deal of time emphasising the expensiveness of advertising in the Magazine compared to other media. The implications obviously were that the advertising department had done well to sell as much as they had, and that perhaps the rate should be brought down.

If it were indeed true that the page rate was unacceptably high to advertisers, then in view of the cost structure the only sensible conclusion at this point should have been that the medium itself was too expensive to be viable. If it couldn't be sold at an economic price, then there was no point in persevering with it: an advertising page had to be sold at a price that covered the cost of producing it plus the cost of producing, roughly speaking, a page of editorial. Otherwise there was no point in the exercise.

But that argument wasn't made. The committee considered briefly the advantages of closure, which were simply the elimination of forecast loss (offset by redundancy costs which were estimated at anywhere from £160,000 to £1 million – the high figure being based on paying one year's salary per head to people who had only been working for five months.)

Then it looked at the arguments for continuing. It stressed the need for maintaining *Mirror* circulation, then beginning to be affected by Murdoch's *Sun*, though there was little evidence that the Magazine was inducing anyone to buy the *Mirror*, and none that it induced people to buy it on the five days a week the magazine didn't appear.

It pointed out that retailers would lose some money if the Magazine closed, and that the printing unions would also be displeased (in spite of the year's pay per man offer). Either group might, the committee feared, take retaliatory action against other parts of IPC.

It raised again the old strategic arguments. If there was no *Mirror* Magazine another paper (presumably from Murdoch's stable) might launch one, though it seems unlikely that the *Mirror's* failure would actually encourage anyone else to try. And the *Mirror* wouldn't be offering anything to compete with colour television (though demonstrably IPC would, through its existing magazines – but the idea of treating IPC as a corporate whole was still a fairly revolutionary one).

And it finally pointed out that closure would be an overt admission of failure and misjudgement that would, putting it mildly, react adversely on the credibility of IPC senior management.

It's an interesting thought that continuing to lose millions could be seen as better for the corporation's image than swiftly cutting its losses. In the newspaper world, however, it makes some kind of sense. If you stave off admitting failure, and cross your fingers hard enough, the miracle may happen and you may never have to admit it.

So the report recommended continuation, and the Board agreed. Not unconditionally, however. The decision taken was to reconsider the position in October 1970, when more accurate information would be available. In the meantime, more money would be spent on promotion, the sales force would be strengthened, the quality of colour would be improved, more market research would be commissioned. And there would be an attempt to reduce printing costs. Pointedly, there was no suggestion that there should be any management changes.

In the upshot of course, the money was spent but the costs not reduced. Then, in April 1970, IPC was taken over by the then Reed Paper Group, and the new management, with rather stronger control over the divisions, rather harder heads, and, perhaps above all, no fear of damaging their own image, closed the Magazine in July . . . about as soon as was practically possible.

None of the feared consequences followed. Nobody else launched a popular magazine supplement, nobody struck and retailers didn't black other IPC magazines. And while *Mirror* circulation went into decline against *The Sun*, there's no reason to suppose that the colour magazine would have altered the trend.

As it transpired, the magazine had lost a fraction under £2 million in the five months 1969/70, and was now forecast (by Reed) to be heading for the £3 million loss in 1970/71 which could have been projected as early as February.

Naturally enough, the closure was accompanied by a great deal of public dispute and autopsy. The Magazine was said to have been launched at the wrong time, to have carried too little editorial (!), to have carried unsuitable editorial. It was even suggested that the advertising rate should have been lower . . . to attract more advertising. Even the fact that the Magazine was known to be doing badly was blamed: the marketing service director of Leo Burnett-LPE (Simon Broadbent) was quoted by *Campaign* as saying: 'If Ryder had made a public statement guaranteeing the magazine for a period of something like two years, it would have brought in £500,000 in advertising revenue that week.'

That may have been true. But it seems likely that the Reed management had realised what still seemed beyond the power of anyone in Fleet Street to imagine: that every pound of advertising revenue was costing something over two pounds to get. Sensibly they gave up the battle, believing, probably correctly, that the struggle to get a still higher page rate was not worth while, in view of the antagonism not so much of the buyers as of the salesman.

Essentially, that decision (not to go ahead, rather than to close) should have been taken as soon as the original page rate (of £8,800) was reduced. It may have been true that no one was going to pay that much for a page of colour advertising: but if it was true then there was no case for going ahead with the Magazine at all. It was doomed from that point to lose more money then IPC could afford, and much more than could possibly justify the intangible strategic benefits that were hoped for. It should have been stopped. But it wasn't. And the most outstanding example of a Fleet Street loss took place.

Egregious though it may have been, the story of the *Mirror* Magazine still provides lessons that are important to anyone trying to understand the financial and economic situation of Fleet Street and the attitudes of the managements responsible for its fortunes.

Of some importance is the way in which the editorial nature of the Magazine rather than its economics was allowed to dictate how it was managed (and to influence the choice of managers). A related failure was not to realise that the editorial criteria which have been evolved for selling newspapers do not apply to a publication intended to be given away.

Thus the Magazine from the outset had all the trappings of an independent publication. It had for instance its own 'agony column' (duplicating, with variations, the one in the *Mirror* itself) and other regular features. In newspapers generally, these things act to reinforce the habit of buying: in a supplement they are essentially unnecessary.

No consideration was ever given to evolving an editorial format to fit the circumstances of the Magazine – to developing it as an effective supplement to the *Mirror*, rather than as a kind of parasitic rival. The belief that a magazine is a magazine and everyone knows what goes into a magazine led to the creation of something which looked like a thin and insubstantial competitor with the rest of the newsagent's display.

There was, too, the continuing preoccupation with total advertising revenue, without counting the profitability of this revenue, coupled with the introduction of a page rate set by the same criteria which determined the *Daily Mirror's* rate structure, oblivious to the fact that *Daily Mirror* advertising was then as now subsidised by circulation revenue.

Standing out from anything else is, of course, the preoccupation with status and image. In hindsight, there can be no doubt that the attraction of the *Mirror* Magazine to the IPC management was largely that of the statue to Pygmalion, Gallipoli to Winston Churchill, or the Sistine roof to Michelangelo. Or the Concorde to BAC. Had it succeeded, the *Mirror* Magazine would have been (it could at least have been presented as) one of the major publishing achievements of recent decades.

Now susceptibility to the attractions of personal achievement and glory is unimpeachable, even in business, when the money at risk belongs to the risker. If the loss on the launch of the *Sunday Telegraph* (itself motivated more by the simple desire to own an influential Sunday paper rather than any search for more money) had resulted in losses of tens of millions rather than hundreds of thousands, there would have been no ground for criticism of the Berry family. It was their own money.

Once public shareholding becomes widespread, however, accountability changes. And one of the keys to an understanding of Fleet Street is to recognise that it still acts as if newspapers were the personal property of Press lords. This is not only true of managements which still treat chairmen and managing directors with the subservience that in other industries is normally reserved for those who can back their position with shareholdings. It is equally true of unions and staff whose antagonisms, verbal and behavioural, are, as I will be discussing in later chapters, essentially of an old-fashioned kind.

The same strand of sensitivity to personal image is evident from the continuing reluctance to kill the magazine, which reached its peak in the Board decision of February 1970. But an equally important strand is the timidity which was displayed against various outside threats. There was the ever-present fear of union action, and the consequent readiness to offer redundancy payments six or seven times as great as those normal in the industry. Similarly, there was the fear that retailers and distributors might take retaliatory action against other IPC publications, although IPC publications at the time accounted for the bulk of most retailers' turnover.

In the event, neither of these fears materialised. But, again, no one is going to understand Fleet Street who doesn't take into account the timidity that dominates most Fleet Street decision-making where there is a chance of conflict either with the unions or with any of the commercial or financial organisations on which it depends. (To its credit, Fleet Street has usually displayed no such timidity on the editorial side in facing up to governmental pressures, or even to pressure from advertisers. But that recurrent courage contrasts markedly with the prevalent commercial attitudes.)

A similar timidity was obviously at the root of the problem over advertising page rates. Salesmen in any industry have an inbuilt tendency to push the price of their product as low as possible in order to make selling easier. But Fleet Street is, if not uniquely, at least unusually ready to accept salesmen's decisions in such instances. And that readiness is more than anything a reflection of the industry's view of itself as commercially dependent on, and therefore subservient to, the advertiser. What is missing, at least since the end of newsprint rationing, is any recognition that advertisers are still more dependent on newspapers than newspapers are on advertising. Despite that, the industry cringes before the advertiser.

It also of course cringes before the unions: but this particular situation is so central to the entire Fleet Street predicament that it warrants several chapters. In moving on to it, however, I can only point to the cautionary tale of the *Mirror* Magazine as some evidence that, even granted harmonious labour relations, Fleet Street might still be a pretty sick place.

5

Earnings

Anyone browsing through official statistics on employment and earnings might be forgiven for wondering why there is any fuss about the newspaper industry. For instance there is no cause for shock in the table issued by the Department of Employment (DEP) in 1970 for growth in basic weekly and hourly rates, as the sample in Table 1 shows. Over the fourteen years, 1956–70, basic weekly rates in the 'publishing, printing and paper-making' industries were up by 98 per cent; hourly rates were up by 116 per cent and hours worked down by 9·3 per cent. By comparison, the manufacturing industries' averages were up by 94·6 per cent, up by 115·2 per cent and down by 9·6 per cent respectively.

Indeed, of the eighteen categories of industry listed in the full DEP table, publishing, printing and paper-making come fifth for increase in weekly rates, eighth for increase in hourly rates, and sixteenth for decrease in hours worked. Better than average, maybe, but nothing very much to shout about.

Of course, there are two obvious and immediate objections to this particular set of figures. In the first place it only shows growth, and gives no indication of actual earnings and hours worked; in the second, the publishing, printing and paper-making classification is an unduly broad one: Fleet Street earnings could well be masked by those of workers elsewhere in the country.

Again, however, looking at the Ministry statistics for actual earnings doesn't reveal anything obviously exceptional: Table 2 samples the figures from the 1970 compilation. On weekly earnings, the industry does now come top, with £33·68; but only barely ahead of motor industry workers with £32·43. On hourly earnings they still fall behind the motor-workers with 74·35p to 76·49p – mainly because of their apparently longer than average working week. In fact, the hours worked, at 45·4, put them thirteenth of 23 categories, moderately worse off than the all-industry average of 44·9 hours.

TABLE 1

BASIC WEEKLY AND HOURLY RATES IN BRITISH INDUSTRY, 1970

Category	Weekly pay	Hourly pay	Hours worked
Paper, print, publishing	198	216	91·7
Transport & communications	212	239	88·8
Gas, electricity, water	211	233	90·6
Bricks, pottery, glass	210	232	90·6
Chemicals & allied	198	215	91·8
Food, drink, tobacco	197	221	89·1
Metals	196	216	90·9
Textiles (worst in list)	180	203	88·9
All manufacturing industries	194·6	215·2	90·4

Index: 1956=100

TABLE 2

AVERAGE EARNINGS AND HOURS WORKED, OCTOBER 1970

Category	Weekly	Hourly	Hours worked
Paper, print, publishing	£33·68	74·35p	45·3
Vehicles	32·43	76·49	42·4
Coal & petroleum	30·82	70·05	44·0
Shipbuilding	29·59	65·32	45·3
Bricks, pottery, glass	28·72	61·24	46·9
Construction	26·85	56·53	47·5
Gas, electricity, water	26·02	59·14	44·0
All manufacturing industries	28·91	64·39	44·9
(Newspaper workers	39·55	89·28	44·3)

Source: *DEP Yearbook*.

TABLE 3

DISTRIBUTION OF GROSS WEEKLY EARNINGS IN SOME SKILLED
TRADES, 1970

Trade	Lower decile	Lower quart.	Median	Upper quart.	Upper decile
Compositors	£21·9	26·3	31·2	39·8	50·4
Press operatives	20·2	24·3	31·3	38·9	47·2
Miner (underground)	18·0	23·7	27·1	29·9	35·1
Skilled welder	22·7	26·3	31·2	37·7	46·2
Steel erector	24·7	29·1	34·0	42·7	52·7
Dockers	24·7	29·9	36·0	44·1	53·4
Systems analyst/ programmers	24·0	28·9	35·2	43·6	50·4
Manual men	17·2	20·8	25·6	31·3	37·7
Non-manual men	19·4	24·2	31·4	41·1	55·0
All men	17·8	21·7	27·2	34·5	43·7

Even focusing more sharply on the newspaper industry in particular, while it improves the figures slightly, does not produce anything
immediately abnormal. The figures become £39·55 for weekly
earnings, 44·3 for hours worked, and 89·28p for hourly earnings:
less in fact than the same figures for the printing of periodicals.

One can look even more closely at the situation, and compare the
earnings of two of the skilled newspaper trades, compositors and
press operatives, with some other trades in other industries which
prima facie one might expect to be at much the same level: again,
Table 3 samples the official statistics. Taking the median figure for
earnings, both trades are worse off than steel erectors, programmers,
and dockers: much the same is true even if one takes the upper
decile.

According to the official figures therefore, skilled printers would
seem to fall into much the same category as skilled welders and
slightly behind steel erectors. That doesn't sound too unreasonable.

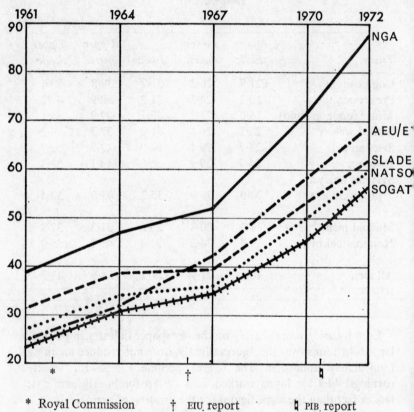

CHART 1

COMPARATIVE GROWTH OF WEEKLY EARNINGS IN PRODUCTION UNIONS

* Royal Commission   † EIU report   ◘ PIB report

NATSOPA includes only mechanical branches.

Only major change in differentials is that achieved by the AEU/ETU.

The acceleration of the second half of the chart covers the period of productivity deals and the introduction of comprehensive wages in many areas.

TABLE 4

SAMPLE OF ACTUAL EARNINGS IN FLEET STREET, FEBRUARY 1973

Occupation	Individual newspapers										Average*
Compositors	—	—	93	—	65	—	124	119	—	83	87
Readers	—	—	76	73	59	114	88	88	70	52	—
Readers' assistants	71	—	63	56	46	82	—	88	—	74	—
Process	59	91	—	97	75	—	73	51	—	65	—
Machine managers	—	69	63	95	47	—	—	83	—	53	—
Machine assistants	—	70	—	76	—	75	—	—	—	—	—
Engineers	81	69	—	—	72	—	75	—	83	83	—
Electricians	—	65	—	—	54	61	—	—	44	85	—
Publishing	—	—	—	—	—	71	91	—	67	—	—
Stereotyping	121	78	64	81	—	63	—	—	—	67	—
Wire-room	—	49	70	—	—	66	63	61	—	—	—
Darkroom	—	43	—	54	—	—	66	49	—	—	—
Average*	71	59	74	86	59	66	73	82	56	66	

Figures are average weekly gross earnings in pounds for employees of each newspaper. Each column represents one daily or evening newspaper. Blank cells indicate either that the information was unavailable, or that the category of employee does not exist on that paper, or that I have suppressed it in order to make identification of the paper harder.

*Including suppressed data. In suppressing I have ensured that, in each line, there remain the highest and lowest items, together with the median (or the two on either side of the median).

So why should one Sunday paper in Fleet Street employ, not as a craftsman but as a messenger, a man who gave up steel erecting because he could make more money carrying pieces of paper around a newspaper office? And why did these passages from the evidence submitted to the last Royal Commission on the Press go unchallenged, even by the unions?

'Earnings in the industry generally are at a very high level indeed.'
Daily Mirror

'These factors have resulted in a high standard of earnings by the production operatives.' *Associated Newspapers*

'Many of them have enjoyed for many years earnings far beyond the level of what has been called a living wage. . . . Many publishers are faced with unrealistic staffing and excessive earnings.'
Thomson Newspapers

'This has led to high wages and inefficiencies.' *The Guardian.*

To move to possibly less biased sources, how could the Economist Intelligence Unit say, in 1966:

'The general level of pay in the Newspaper Industry is out of all proportion to the effort expended and the skill employed compared with most other industries.'

and the Prices and Incomes Board report, in 1970:

'Earnings are very much higher than in manufacturing industry generally, averaging in 1968 (the latest year for which figures are available) approximately £48 per week for craft workers and £42 per week for non-craft workers.'

Unfortunately, obtaining accurate figures for the industry is not easy: for reasons I'll be coming too shortly, it may even be impossible. None are published, and even the Economist Intelligence Unit's otherwise illuminating report quoted no individual earnings figures. As I have mentioned in the preface, getting figures is a matter of approaching individual managements, and, unofficially, trade union officials and individual managers, and rather painstakingly assembling them – which I spent most of my time doing in the first half of 1973.

The figures I have are not therefore a hundred per cent guaranteed.

In an industry where in some places even the management does not know accurately from week to week what is being paid to whom, a hundred per cent is perhaps too much to ask for anyway. But none of these figures have been challenged by anyone I have shown them to, in union or management.

Some of these figures are tabulated in Chart 1 and Table 4. In 1970 average production wages appear to have come to £52·93 per week, ranging from just over £64 for compositors to just over £40 for proof-pullers and copy-holders. By 1972, the average had moved up to £64·50, with compositors up to £80 (piece-workers were averaging nearer £90). The only group still below £50 at the time were dark-room workers.

Those figures refer, fairly closely, to the time when the then government introduced its wage freeze. Fleet Street being Fleet Street, by the time the wage freeze ended in the early spring of 1973, there had already been a general increase of 8 per cent (the story of which is told in Chapter 4), and, it would appear, a further drift of 1–2 per cent all round, with, in one or two places, a significantly greater rise still.

Obviously, such variances (and such apparent confusion) have explanations. That basic rates, as opposed to earnings, are not very relevant is hardly surprising: in most industries, basic rates are complicated by local agreements and the incidence of overtime, though I suspect it must be fairly rare that someone on a basic rate of around £23 a week, like some stereotypers at the time of writing, can take home over £100 a week without even being on piece-work. But even so, official statistics are supposed to take that sort of thing into account. The reasons why they apparently do not, or not sufficiently, are perhaps surprisingly not all that hard to find: the only real difficulty comes from suspending one's disbelief long enough to accept that some of the reasons are real, and not the product of satirical fiction. They can be separated, at least roughly, into four kinds, although there are some inevitable overlaps. To each of them I have devoted a section of this chapter: for three of the four of them I have stuck to their colloquial names, partly because they are succinct and colourful, partly because to provide formal circumlocutions would lend a spurious air of rationality to a system which is nothing of the kind.

'GHOST' WORKING

Until 1961, the *Sunday Times* was produced on the presses of the

Daily Telegraph in Fleet Street. For reasons immaterial to this story, its production was then moved to Thomson House in Gray's Inn Road, a move that, naturally enough, involved a flurry of trade union negotiations before it could be consummated. One of the issues involved is of particular interest.

If the paper had remained at the *Daily Telegraph*, its production would have required an extra machine, thanks to the boom in circulation it was experiencing at the time. The union therefore claimed that an extra machine, eight instead of seven, should also be used at Thomson House, to cope with the extra print. In fact, the Thomson House machines were newer, and it was empirically obvious that the seven could cope: and in any case only seven were available. It takes time to order and deliver a printing press. Since the union was perfectly capable of appreciating this, it proposed that to compensate for the lack of the extra machine, a payment equal to the wages of an extra crew should be made, and shared out between the men working.

In practice, management conceded the claim, though in principle it did not concede the argument. According to their evidence to the Royal Commission they paid the money 'in recognition of the conditions in the Machine Room during the present period of reconstruction and machine installation'. But whatever the theoretical argument, Fleet Street had gained another 'ghost' crew.

The same shift of production had another similar effect. At the *Daily Telegraph*, in some departments the *Sunday Times* had been produced by a special staff. In others, its production had been carried out by members of the *Daily Telegraph* staff who were paid extra for the extra work involved. In particular this was true of the process department and the wire-room.

Not unnaturally, when they heard of the approaching departure of the *Sunday Times*, the process workers were apprehensive. Their union representatives met with the management, and were reassured that with the launch of the *Sunday Telegraph*, which was already being planned, there was no reason for them to worry. Management was prepared to guarantee no loss of earnings. The union was satisfied, and management too: not unreasonably, since the *Sunday Telegraph*, at least in its early days, used more blocks, albeit smaller ones, than the *Sunday Times*. There was genuinely no diminution of work.

However, the wire-room staff, hearing of the guarantee given to the process department, asked for the same guarantee. And were given it. Which might not seem to matter, save for the fact that the *Sunday Times*, like the *Daily Telegraph*, was printed in Manchester as well as in London, and the bulk of the wire-room work was concerned with the transmission of messages, pictures, and copy between the two offices. The *Sunday Telegraph* was not planned to be printed in Manchester, and still is not. It therefore has no call for anything like the same number of staff. Nonetheless it has the same number. The wire-room staff of the *Daily Telegraph* still 'works' a full Saturday shift for the *Sunday Telegraph*. 'Works' naturally in quotation marks. Since both sides are pragmatic enough to accept the practical situation, the staff simply come in on a rota which roughly averages one half-shift a month. And get paid for four full Saturdays. (Ironically enough, though this is not the reason, the *Daily Telegraph* wire-room is anyway the highest paid in the industry.)

For the first five years of its existence I worked for the *Sunday Telegraph* myself, and was in and out of the wire-room every Saturday without realising that any of this was happening: not till I started this investigation did I find out. That there were usually only one or two people working in a room lined with a couple of dozen assorted keyboards seemed natural enough since the machines were there for the *Daily Telegraph*. There was no way of telling that the apparently idle machines were actually manned by intangible spirits.

Neither of these two situations is in any way isolated. The argument that more machinery was required (to produce bigger papers) and that, since it was not available, the men working should be paid the wages of those that should be was also used at *The People*, at least in Manchester: the more common argument that more men are required (either to handle extra work, or to maintain official manning standards), and that, since there are none available, those working should be paid the wages of those only doing so in theory, has been used almost everywhere. In the *Daily Telegraph*, at least in the early 'sixties, in the machine-room for a 28-page paper, the official manning figure was 306. The figure itself was only accepted with some reluctance by management, reluctance presumably intensified by the fact that the department was regularly manned by 252 men, who shared the other 54 pay packets between them.

Multiplying instances might be amusing, but hardly of great value. Putting a figure on the contribution that 'ghost' working makes to the overall disparity between notional and actual earnings would still remain an impossible task. It is still evidently a substantial if inestimable contribution to the average pay-packet.

This is true even though some papers in the later 'sixties managed to conclude 'productivity' deals with some of the chapels by which some of the more grossly anomalous payments were included in a 'comprehensive' wage. Perhaps the proportion of earnings made up by 'ghost' working is today lower than for some years past. What is important however is that the principle is well established, and while the unions retain power on the one hand to set high manning standards for machinery and to restrict its output, and on the other hand to restrict availability of manpower below what those standards dictate, then 'ghosts' will form an inevitable part of the working population of Fleet Street.

'BLOW' SYSTEMS

To 'take a blow' is a common-or-garden English idiom for to take a rest, and rest periods are an obviously necessary concomitant of any work system. Even the strictest of Taylorian industrial engineers agree that the worker needs and is entitled to his 'blow'.

But that is not quite the way it works out in Fleet Street.

For instance, the union-management agreed 'blow' for a worker in the *Sunday Mirror* publishing department is one hour in three: overtly, perhaps a little excessive, but maybe not astonishingly so. However, since the war the job itself, bundling, tying and despatching the papers, has been largely mechanised, with only a slight reduction in staff (to handle two million copies in 1939 took 189 men: five million in 1970 took 400). A rest system designed for an environment in which an adequate staff was working continuously is therefore apparently projected into a situation in which men are already underemployed. And there are other complications.

For the work-load is by no means continuous. It peaks irregularly with each edition, which can't be parcelled until it starts coming off the machines, and must be finished in time to catch the trains taking it to the area it is destined for. Between peaks there are lulls in which the department as a whole is resting anyway. The basic shift is seven hours, and overtime is normally worked: the effective time spent packing the *Sunday Mirror* is not much more than five hours.

Unfortunately, both from the point of view of labour costs and the rationality of the system, individual 'blows' are not synchronised with the lulls, but stick religiously to the one-man-off-for-two-on schedule. In theory. In practice the men 'off' at peak times are normally needed to cope with the extra load, which they do in return for being paid an overtime hour.

I chose the *Sunday Mirror* as an example mainly because it is easier to compare staffing figures with pre-war: changes in the length of the working week become immaterial. But essentially the same system applies to the *Daily Mirror*, and indeed to all other publishing departments.

A nominal 35-hour week therefore, on a daily paper, is transformed with eleven hours 'blow', of which say six are worked, into a nominal 41-hour week with six of them at overtime rates. Only thirty however, are, actually worked. On the assumption of an average £1 an hour (chosen for arithmetical simplicity), the result is a week's pay of £44: average hourly earnings are reported as £1·07 instead of the true £1·47. The figures may or may not of course be further increased by 'ghost' payments, or actual overtime (i.e. hours worked outside the 35-hour basic).

From office to office, and department to department, the arrangements for 'blow' vary in detail, but the system remains essentially the same in most places, the only major exception being among compositors, since most work on a piece-work basis.

The effect in one machine-room provides a succinct example of the results of the system. The original data are from the EIU report, though the calculations are my own.

On one measured five-hour machine run, the number of man-hours actually worked came to 35·6, though that figure may be considered a little harsh, since it results from multiplying the number of men working by the minutes they were working for. Crediting a man with an hour's work if he did any work at all in the hour, the figure comes to 46. The number of man-hours *attended* i.e., the number of men present multiplied by the time they were present for, came to 66·2. The number of official man-hours, i.e., the number of men being paid to be there multiplied by the time they were supposed to be there came to 115·75. Official 'blow' therefore amounted to 49·55 hours: 43 per cent. What most people would consider 'blow' (time not working) came to 80·15 hours: 69 per cent.

Whether any of the men employed on that machine for that shift also received payment for 'ghosts' notionally working elsewhere, I do not know. But it's evident enough that the 'blow' system contributes its share to the discrepancy between reported and actual hourly earnings. It does not however obviously contribute to the discrepancy between reported and actual weekly earnings. That it can do so indirectly is because of the contribution it makes to the practice which is the subject of the next section.

DOUBLE-WORKING

Among the unavoidable peculiarities of Fleet Street, indeed all, newspaper production is the fact that the work-load varies enormously from day to day. This is a truism in the case of the Sunday papers and the odd weekly extras, from *Reveille* to the *Times Literary Supplement,* which crowd the vast bulk of production into one day.

But it is also true of the daily papers, visibly so even to the casual reader in the case of pagination: Friday's papers are large, Saturday's and Monday's small. That circulation also varies considerably in a weekly cycle may not be so visible, but is just as true: indeed it is the reason, ultimately, for the difference in number of pages. As a result, most Fleet Street papers are reliant on casual workers, paid by the shift, and working one, two, three shifts a week. Some work four, but in many Fleet Street departments, four shifts a week is full-time. So institutionalised is the practice that there are two recognised classes of casuals: 'regular casuals', employed on a more-or-less long-term agreement, and with certain holiday and welfare entitlements, and 'casual casuals', hired from day to day (through the union, it may be worth pointing out here).

The demand for casuals is increased by the practice of some newspapers of employing men on a per-shift basis even for routine activities. Thus on *The Sun*, which has some 50 full-time stereotypers, a further 25 or so are regularly employed on a casual basis.

Now, even under the Industrial Relations Act, there was no question of Fleet Street managements employing outside labour for such jobs, no matter how unskilled, even when union labour was unavailable. (Anyone who thinks there might be has missed the point of 'ghost' working: if the required extra hands are not available, the men already employed do the work and get paid extra for it.) Coupling this tight control on supply with the existing demand, it becomes obvious that anyone working in Fleet Street can boost his weekly earnings with a night or two's casual work, whenever he feels like it. Actually, 'anyone' is a bit too strong. For instance, compositors employed by one paper are specifically barred, by their union, from working for another. This is a ruling that dates back to the craft origins of the trade, and does not arouse the resentment one might have suspected. It does however mean that their members feel freer to talk about the system than members of some other unions.

Moreover, it is obviously easier for someone working on a daily paper to do an extra shift for a Sunday paper than vice-versa, since the Sunday demand is so much greater. This occasionally does appear to cause some resentment, most of which however is mollified by the fact that Sunday paper rates for regulars tend to be higher.

What such extra shifts are paid of course varies enormously, from paper to paper as well as from department to department. One daily paper pays its casual stereotypers £17 for a nine-hour shift: on the publishing side it pays outdoor workers £15 and indoor £13·50. One Sunday pays its ('regular') casual stereotypers anything from £18 to £28 depending on hours worked, which nominally range from eight to fourteen. On the publishing side it pays outdoor and indoor staff £27·10 and £26·90 respectively, while in the machine-room it pays assistants from £22 to £30, though technically for an 18-hour day.

It is difficult to establish any kind of overall pattern. By and large Saturday casuals seem to get about twice as much per shift as mid-week ones, for a nominally much longer day: though the previous section has indicated how much reliance can be placed on reported hours worked. Again, while this may seem to place Fleet Street workers in a happy position, it may not seem much to get excited about. Earning extra by 'moonlighting' is a fairly common and acceptable way of boosting one's income. But two factors combine to alter the picture somewhat.

The first is the effect of the 'blow' system (and over-manning generally) in normal working time. It is at least arguable that men who were fully employed in their normal working time, and being paid a reasonable sum for it, would not be so eager to take on extra commitments: nor would they perhaps be so willing to if the extra work they were taking on was itself laborious. After all, we are not confronted here by someone on a poverty-line £20 a week desperately trying to increase it to a bearable £30.

The second factor is even less defensible, and is again made possible only by the blow system and by over-manning. This is the undeniable situation in which casuals, particularly on Saturday, but also on other days of the week, sign on for shifts with two papers at the same time. Officially of course it doesn't happen. But too many people on the union side are willing to talk about it for its occurrence to be seriously disputed. Sometimes it is a question of working for one paper while on 'blow' from the other, and vice-versa: the EIU observed at the *News of the World* that in some departments there were more people idle than working so it is not impossible. More frequently however it appears to be a case of turning up and signing on, then leaving and only coming back later to collect the pay-packet. This practice is of course helped by the government ruling that part-time workers only have to have insurance cards stamped by the first employer of the week. Fleet Street employers therefore, no matter what influence they have on the number of men they employ, have neither control nor check on *whom* they employ. Whatever name the man gives on signing on has to be accepted, and the pay-packet made out (and tax returns and official statistics made out) on the basis of that name. The Fred Smith working for the *Sunday Telegraph* this Saturday may therefore also be the Joe Bloggs working for the *News of the World* (I choose these two papers deliberately: several FoCs (Fathers of Chapels) assure me that double-working between these two papers is more common than between any other pair, though I cannot be sure it is true). And no one knows except Fred/Joe Smith/Bloggs himself.

It only adds the final touch of comedy never very far away from any Fleet Street labour situation to point out that apparently from time to time even Smith/Bloggs does not know. A small, but noticeable, number of casual pay-packets once in a while go uncollected in Fleet Street offices. Which is difficult to account for except on the basis usually advanced by Fleet Street managers: that the man concerned had forgotten the name he had used to sign on.

FIDDLES AND THE LIKE
It may seem that this would be a suitable heading under which to have treated the subject of double working. I have however reserved it for two classes of activity. The first is that of activities which both sides of the industry would recognise as being in a sense illegitimate (which isn't to say they would necessarily frown on it), and would admit to be so if a particular case were made public. And the second is simply a rag-bag for including several devices which, while officially

supported by the union, or at least the chapel, are nevertheless simply manoeuvres for boosting earnings without doing any extra work.

In the first category, an undoubted fiddle, and therefore one not publicly admitted to happen, is the situation in which a compositor (on piece-work) sets, say, a headline in which there is subsequently discovered to be a mistake. Officially, the mistake should be spotted by the proof-readers, and sent back for correction, for which the compositor gets paid again. That's the system, not the fiddle. The fiddle comes (or at least the opportunity for it comes) when the correction is independently spotted by someone on the editorial staff, and the necessary alteration sent down by him as well as the one sent by the readers. In that case the compositor can get to charge for the same correction twice, while only doing it once.

Incidentally, in the system of allowing compositors to charge for the correction of their own mistakes there is an obvious opportunity for the making of deliberate errors. It is significant however that I have never heard this alleged, which in the state of endemic distrust in Fleet Street probably means it never happens. This is not so odd as it may seem: to commit errors deliberately, whether to make work or not, would infringe the sense of craft responsibility which, as I will be discussing in the chapters on attitudes, is still powerful in Fleet Street.

For another instance, there is one paper in which, until recently, the messengers were paid a comprehensive wage for a five-day week. Among themselves, however, they had organised an unofficial rota which meant that they only worked for four of the five days. Then they negotiated a new agreement with management that recognised that a four-day week was sufficient, and agreed a new comprehensive wage of £44. Within forty-eight hours, the group had organised for themselves a three-day rota. Here, the comic touch came when the messengers' rota (they would not claim to be experts in work organisation) broke down a week or so after the start, with the result that one day no one turned up for work at all. This was an error that could hardly go unnoticed, and in fact a considerable flap followed, with senior management expostulating with the FoC. Nothing else happened however: the three-day rota still operates.

Finally, under the heading perhaps of fiddles-that-may-or-may-not-be, it is worth noting that in a number of offices in a number of departments, the responsibility for making out pay-slips is not borne by the accounts department, nor yet by a supervisor or a union official. The men make out their own. That is to say, each week each man makes out a statement, sometimes according to one observer 'with a great deal of pondering and pencil-licking', of the number of hours he has worked and the rate at which they should be charged, and hands it in. The accounts department then makes up the pay-packet. Whether or not that actually leads to fiddles, nobody knows.

Unlike these examples, the second category (the 'like' of the section heading) is not considered disreputable, and is usually hallowed either by tradition or official union sanction. However, it shares with pure 'fiddles' the common essence of resulting in payment for not working.

The oldest and best established example is undoubtedly the money earned by compositors for 'fat'. Once upon a time, all material carried in a newspaper was set in type by the newspaper's staff, being paid for, as now, mostly on a piece basis. However, with the growing professionalisation of advertising, it has become more and more common for space advertisements (i.e., anything outside 'classified') to be supplied by the advertising agent in the form of a line or half-tone or hybrid block, or stereo plate. No setting therefore needs to be done: the supplied plate is merely inserted into the forme. In the case of a full-page advertisement, obviously, no imposition needs to be carried out either, but since the compositors who handle imposition are normally paid on a time basis, they are unaffected. The piece-work compositors, however, saw this practice originally as a threat to their incomes, if not exactly to their livelihood. It was therefore opposed, and settlement reached on the basis that staff would be paid an amount of money equivalent to that which would have been paid if the material had been set 'in-house'. Such money is 'fat': it is paid into a pool and shared out among the members. This is one of the customs hallowed by tradition. But it is also backed by a typical Fleet Street rationalisation: 'if we insisted on doing it our-selves they'd have to pay us, so why should we lose if we let them use stereos?'

Tradition has less of a role in another example of the not-quite-fiddle, though it still plays a part. There is a clause in the standard NPA/PKTF agreement which says:

VI: Change-over to Summer-time
On the night of the change-over from GMT [Greenwich mean time] to summer-time, or from summer-time to double-summer-time, the

clocks shall be deemed to be advanced at the end of the night's attendance.* If, owing to the times of publication and/or trains, it is necessary in any office to call men in earlier and/or for men to work through meal times, the usual conditions for starting work earlier or for working through meal times shall apply.

The rest of Britain changes its clocks at 2 a.m.: i.e., at 2 a.m. the hands of the clock are moved forward immediately to 3 a.m. As a result, were it not for the above agreement, someone coming on at 10 p.m. and working eight hours would find himself leaving, not at 6 a.m., but at 7. In view of the agreement however, the NPA assumes that he is only entitled to eight hours' pay. However, in March 1968, the *Sunday Express* publishing chapel claimed an hour's overtime pay for each man involved (for 'working on an hour'). Under threat of a stoppage, management paid. In 1969, '70 and '71 the matter didn't arise since the government was experimenting with having 'summer' time all the year round. In 1972 the experiment was dropped however, and in both 1972 and 1973 the claim was made again, this time with the extra argument that a precedent had been established. Each time the claim was met by management, and will presumably continue to be paid.

On another paper, another chapel, the stereotypers, also claimed an extra hour's pay (at overtime rate) in 1973 because the change-over to summer-time altered the time of their meal break. The management decided to pay, and argue later. However, on the Friday (the change-over to summer-time is always on a Sunday morning) the management informed the NPA, who talked to the union at branch level. Branch told the chapel to withdraw the claim, not as it happens on the ground that the claim was silly, but on the ground that the management had given the chapel a week's notice of the change, therefore conforming with the stereotypers' national agreement on the procedure with regard to meal times.

If formal notice had not been given – if, that is, management had relied on the normal government-sponsored notice given to the public at large – presumably the claim would have been pressed, the payment made 'under duress', and yet another precedent set.

SUMMARY
Hopefully, this short tour around some of the major oddities of

* In some industries it would say 'night's work'.

the Fleet Street pay structure helps to account for the question I started out with: the discrepancy between the image of the over-paid and under-employed newspaper worker and the figures in the official statistics. It is obvious that the basic pay level is entirely irrelevant. In fact when basic pay was as low as £16–17 a worker might take home £60–£70, even without double working. A compositor earning well over £100 in the week might well have been doing so on a basic of a little over £20.

It is also apparent that reported earnings may have very little to do with actual earnings: and to use either figure to calculate hourly rates verges on the ridiculous. Admittedly, I have little idea at first-hand how far reported earnings and hours worked in other industries correspond to reality, though I suspect that in few if any does the discrepancy go as far as in Fleet Street. That judgement I can only leave to the reader.

In concentrating on the earnings of individuals I have obviously ignored some factors in the situation which inflate wage-bills without increasing any particular individual's earnings. Manning however is a question more appropriate to the next chapter: all I would like to add here are two quotations, both from the evidence submitted to the Shawcross Royal Commission on the Press. They are therefore now over ten years old: but both are still germane. The first is from the *Daily Mirror*, and is a footnote referring to a tabulated figure (776) for the number employed in the publishing department (including van-drivers):

'Includes 39 men surplus to negotiated mechanical publishing staff who do not physically take part in production.'

The second is even more poignant, and comes from the *Daily Telegraph*, and refers to their process department:

'In this department we pay a "House Extra" of £5 10s per week, but are far from clear what we get for it.'

6

Decisions and controls

To assimilate from the last chapter only that basic rates and reported earnings are minimally related to actual earnings and hours worked would be to miss half its point, and perhaps the more important half: For the major proportion of his earnings, the part represented by 'ghost' payments, 'fat', casual working and so on, the Fleet Street worker is dependent not on management, nor even on management-influenced-by-the-unions, but directly on the unions themselves, and more particularly on the elected father of his chapel.

For the decisions which most immediately affect his take-home pay are made, not by management, but by the union. This is only one aspect of the way in which the trade union organisation has come to exercise much of what is usually, if somewhat plaintively, regarded as the 'management prerogative'. I have tried to separate out the various manifestations of this arrogation according to the traditional classification of management functions in the various sections of this chapter: since the subject has already been introduced, it seems simplest however to start by continuing to discuss earnings.

PAY DECISIONS
Among the compositors, the basic rate of pay is the subject of management-union negotiation, and therefore in some sense still subject to management decision, or at least acquiescence. In the same way, the piece rates that make up most of the compositor's earnings are negotiated between the two. However, as far as the individual compositor is concerned, what work he gets to do, both in amount and kind (some kinds are more profitable than others), and what share he gets of the 'fat' payments, and therefore how his personal pay-packet gets made up, is entirely dependent on the three-way balance between himself, the father of his chapel, and the other members of it. Management has no hand in it at all.

The 'fat' sum in particular is calculated by the FoC, or by someone he asks to do it for him. The job is a laborious one, and is alleged, understandably, to take up the entire time of some FoCs, thereby interfering not only with their composing duties, but more import-antly with their other union duties. Once calculated, and agreed, the money is paid over to the FoC, by the management, and distributed by him to his members. In the division, he has theoretically nothing to guide him but his own sense of fairness. However, he is an elected official: he cannot therefore allow that sense to stray too far from the communal sense of what is proper. (To be fair, most FoCs I have observed carry out such activities with a scrupulousness that appears to stem more from their own rigorous sense of propriety than from the fear of not being re-elected.) Much the same is true of ghost payments in all departments affected by them.

Superficially, it might seem that casual workers are more de-pendent on management for their extra income, but in practice casual work is obtained as the result of a process of bargaining between the chapel and the branch. The FoC normally puts in the request for extra workers to the Branch, which chooses them: I don't know that it has ever happened, but it seems likely that the FoC could object to any particular individual if he or his members wanted to. There is no question of management being able to (except in the case of NATSOPA clerical workers to some extent: I'll return to this shortly). For extra work the man is therefore depen-dent solely on the union.

This is an especially important factor in the union, SOGAT, in which casual work is most widespread. Even among daily papers with a full-time SOGAT staff in the publishing rooms of something just over 1,000, 1,250 casual (regular casual and casual casual) shifts are worked in a week: about a quarter of the work is therefore done by casuals. On the Sunday papers, the vast bulk of the work is of course casual: the *Sunday Mirror* employs not far short of 500 over the week-end, or as mid-week casuals, as opposed to the literal handful it employs full-time. Even allowing for the proportion of regular casual work, which is difficult to estimate, the job allocation problem is therefore obviously a considerable one, especially since it includes arranging for holiday and sickness cover (where this is in fact provided, rather than paid for on a 'ghost' basis). It is entirely handled by the unions.

The opportunity for corruption in such a situation is self-evident. That it can happen has been sufficiently demonstrated in the United States, and, at one time, in some of the British docks. That it happens in Fleet Street, I have no evidence. It is however certainly alleged to happen, not only by management, but by members and officials of other unions, including many with strong left-wing views. Some of the latter believe that it was one of the prime issues on which the merger between NATSOPA and the old Paper-workers' union to form SOGAT was broken by the secession of NATSOPA. If such corruption did exist, however, it would only lend strength to the main point: that for a major part of his income, the worker is dependent, not on management, but on his elective or appointive union officials. Equally, he is dependent on them for the closely related question of how much time he has to work to get the money.

Where shift rotas exist, they are normally prepared by the union: so, too, is overtime allocated. How the 'blow' system works out in detail and in practice, and how it affects particular individuals, is decided by the union: and double working of course would be impossible without the knowledge, if not the connivance, of the FoC. In most departments, too, the system of 'early cuts' operates. When, as not infrequently happens, Fleet Street being manned for peak conditions, there is not enough work available for the staff on hand, the FoC will detail some members to go home early. They are still, naturally, credited with the hours not worked. Something similar happens in many industries: the important thing here is that it is the FoC who decides how many, and who, should go.

(The system, obviously, can create production problems, even though most FoCs operate it with due regard for getting the work out, and in informal consultation with editorial or even management. Thus in *The Times* some years ago, before the present management's time, it was impossible to produce pictures of a late-night train crash because the process department had closed down early, having nothing else to do, and the idea of covering late-night emergencies, at least with pictures, being rather foreign to the traditional culture of *The Times* at that period. Such occasions are, admittedly, rare, and when they happen the people concerned are ready to apologise, though there is of course no question of disciplinary action, and no possibility of rectifying the mistake.)

EMPLOYMENT
The Fleet Street production worker is not only dependent on the union for determining the level of his earnings. He is also dependent on the union for his job itself. If a Fleet Street manager wants to add to his staff, or replace someone (as a result of death, resignation

or retirement, effectively the only ways in which workers leave their jobs), he has to ask the union for a man. In most of the craft unions, most of SOGAT, and in parts of NATSOPA (the darkroom, for instance) the process effectively stops there. The man the union sends gets the job. In theory it might be possible for management to turn the man down, and ask for another: in practice there is such a 'shortage' of craft manpower that it never happens. What does occasionally happen is that the union has no one available, in which case the normal practice, as with casual work, is for the job to be left open, the work being done on a ghost basis.

The area in which this is less rigid in practice, though the system is theoretically roughly the same, is in the NATSOPA clerical branch, which, apart from 'clerks', provides most administrative staff: accountants, computer programmers, advertisement salesmen, even most non-craft managers. Such people are not in the Fleet Street sense of the term 'skilled': however it is accepted that management has a right to insist on candidates being qualified and suitable. So if the union is unable to provide candidates with the required qualifications, frequently the case with some of the more esoteric occupations, the company is allowed to recruit from outside, on condition that the recruit then joins the union.

With that exception, therefore, the worker is dependent on his union for getting the job in the first place. Universally he is also dependent on the union for continuity of employment. If expelled from the union he would be prevented from working (in the case of a craftsman, from working anywhere else that he might get a job), whereas as long as he has union support he is highly unlikely to be fireable by the management.

Perhaps the most significant test-case with regard to management's ability to fire happened in 1954, when a deputy FoC in the *Daily Mirror* machine-room was 'grossly insubordinate' to the Press Room manager, and was given a week's notice. The following night the men refused to produce the paper until he was reinstated. The experience remains a traumatic one in the *Daily Mirror*. At first they were urged by the NPA to stick to their guns and not re-instate the man. Assured that the other daily papers would stick to their informal agreement not to publish if one of their number was in dispute, the *Mirror* agreed. Then, after hasty consultations, at 11 o'clock at night the NPA changed its mind, and asked the *Daily Mirror* to give in and reinstate the man to avoid a national shutdown. The *Mirror* did so, and the principle of job security was established.

That is, of course, job security with union support. Without it, a man can find himself fired, but it doesn't happen very often. It happened once to a machine-room worker who was found to be doing nothing else but make books on horse races, which at the time was illegal (and in those circumstances may still be). Short of actually being caught doing something illegal, it is not easy to lose the support of both sides, though it has begun to happen in recent years in the case of the highly paid: normally journalists, but more and more including 'unskilled' members of NATSOPA clerical.

The only other way it can happen is to be politically or otherwise in conflict with the union. There have been one or two cases of a man being dismissed and failing to get union support against the dismissal, where it is at least alleged that this was because of his political position (too far left, in the only cases of which I have information). This factor loomed large in the minds of some NATSOPA officials recently. NATSOPA, acceding to the TUC's request for demonstrative action against the government on May Day, issued an instruction for strike action to all its branches and chapels. At subsequent chapel meetings, four Fleet Street clerical chapels voted *against* striking, although under the NATSOPA constitution, unlike that of the craft unions, the executive is empowered to order strike action without a ballot. For a few hours, there was a rather heady atmosphere of revolt in the offices concerned, but it vanished over-night, and in the end the 'rebellious' chapels stayed away. (There was even a short period in which it looked as though another flash of Fleet Street comedy might emerge: the doors of one at least of the offices concerned are locked and unlocked by another branch of NATSOPA, and the putative rebels were informed that even if they turned up to work they would find the doors locked against them. Which would at least have given a new twist to the meaning of 'lock-out'.)

In theory, for refusing to strike the members could have been expelled, and that threat obviously weighed strongly with them, but of undoubted equal concern to some of the FoCs involved was the feeling that if they went with their members instead of the union, in any subsequent personal conflict with management they might not be able to rely on exactly 100 per cent support.

The craft unions were in a different position, which will be of more importance in the chapter on attitudes, but is worth briefly mentioning here. Left to itself, their executives too might have decided to support the TUC: but the chapels voted against striking, as earlier they had also voted, against union wishes, to register under the Industrial Relations Act. So they did not take part in the May Day strike. Those of their members who wanted to were nevertheless able to walk in the May Day marches, since the NATSOPA action was enough in itself to close down the papers. But at least they got paid for the day.

Insofar as this total union control over hiring and firing depends on the existence of a closed shop, it theoretically should have changed after the passing of the Industrial Relations Act, which made closed shops illegal except in certain restricted circumstances which did not apply to Fleet Street. In practice however, the Act was ignored by the industry, no matter what may at the time have been hoped by management. In some house agreements concluded after the passing of the Act, the previous formal recognition of the closed shop was deleted: however, most such agreements contained a clause under which the management guaranteed that the closed shop would apply once more when (not if) the Act was repealed – which in 1975 it was.

In general therefore the Industrial Relations Act can be left out of consideration, except insofar as its existence may have affected attitudes on both sides, a subject I will be returning to. In spite of it, it is evident that most of what have been normally considered managerial functions in recruitment, job allocation, firing, and related fields have been arrogated to themselves by the unions. With regard to some of the other areas however it may have been less a case of arrogation by the unions than abandonment by management.

PRODUCTION CONTROL
One NGA FoC, recounting to me the story of one set of negotiations with his management, told of referring to a certain set of output figures for his department. 'How do you know that?' said one of the management team. 'We don't have those figures.' 'All I'd done,' the father of the chapel told me, 'was count up from the filed editions of the paper. *They* could have done that.'

It's possible of course that they had, but were bluffing. I put that thought to him, but he dismissed it. I also put it to him that maybe they were afraid he might object to having his chapel's output measured in this way. He said: 'No, we wouldn't have minded . . . I gave them the figures, didn't I? In any case we would not have known if they had.'

It's easy enough to collect, anecdotally, other such instances. My own departmental output at the *Sunday Telegraph* was never measured in any meaningful way, not even, except in an initial burst of enthusiasm, by me. But perhaps the most telling commentary comes from the Shawcross Royal Commission on the Press.

Not many newspapers in their evidence attempted to give production statistics in detail, but one of those that did was *The Times*. (For the record, I ought to point out that the fullest were given by the papers of the then Mirror Group.) The effect however was somewhat spoilt by continual footnotes to most of the key figures, for instance the number of men employed, the number of plates cast, blocks etched, and so on, explaining that the figures had been 'obtained from the overseer'. Now the overseer, though a union member, is technically a member of management: it's not unreasonable that part of his job should be to provide such figures. What are slightly damning are the two evident implications: that special applications had to be made for them rather than their being available on a routine basis, and that the authors of the evidence were disclaiming any responsibility for their accuracy. That senior management should rely on junior for the provision of statistics is reasonable management practice: that it should absolve itself of responsibility for them is not.

How far astray this lack of production information can lead investigators is, incidentally, indicated by these same *Times* figures, coupled with those provided by the Economist Intelligence Unit four years later. Defeated (self-confessedly) in its attempts to obtain more specific output information, the EIU team was driven to assume that the best available indicator of the output of the process department was the number of editorial pages produced by the paper. (That, and the circulation, which is irrelevant to process work, are statistics which it would be difficult for the newspaper *not* to compile, unless it went to the length of destroying its files.) On doing so, the team (forgivably) seized on the fact that over the period 1957–65 the editorial pages produced by *The Times* had increased by 30 per cent while the process wages costs had increased by 280 per cent.

According to *The Times*' evidence however (as submitted by the overseer) the total number of blocks made *doubled* between 1957

D

and 1961, and the total area of zinc etched (perhaps the best indicator of output, if not of effort expended) went up from 4,303 sq. ins to 11,109, an increase of 260 per cent, or almost as much as wages went up in the EIU's entire eight-year period. In fact, from 1958 to 1961, *The Times* saw an improvement of 28 per cent in wages cost per sq. in. etched, thanks partly to installing new equipment, and partly (from my own memory) to fuller use of existing capacity.

It would be possible to dismiss this as a slip by the EIU, and indeed it was one of the things that provided ammunition for union rejection of the report (if they had needed any). But that would be unfair on the EIU, and in any case would miss the point: the important thing is that the EIU were driven into making it by their knowledge that such figures were not normally available in newspaper offices. Not to management, that is. When it suits their book to produce them, the unions can frequently do so.

The second germane point is that made by my FoC friend above. Sometimes it may be true that management is prevented by the unions from collecting such statistics, as indeed would probably be the case were individuals' figures for output, or even hours worked sought. Frequently however such output statistics are available without the need for union co-operation, but still are not collected, either from a failure to realise their usefulness (even if it is only a question of usefulness in negotiation) or from an unwillingness to run any risk of antagonising the unions.

In 1968, the NPA commissioned a sub-committee to study the problems of applying work study in the industry. One or two quotations from their report illuminate this point considerably.

'Large items of savings are excluded from the areas of productivity bargaining, because no means are available to establish the basic factual data on which management decisions on proposals for improvements can be made. . . .'

'Certain unions have shown objections to work study in the past. It has been deemed sensible to make such savings that are possible in these departments without work study, rather than risking not making savings at all by insisting on work study as a prerequisite.'

This report was made in the rather heady atmosphere that followed the inadvertent publication of the EIU report. It was one of the things that for some of us made the head go flat.

QUALITY CONTROL

While the collection of control statistics, let alone their use, is something that normally for one reason or another goes by default, on the spot quality control is another matter. Compositors may, by tradition as much as anything, work unsupervised, but their output is subject to stringent examination. The proof-readers do nothing else, and roughly speaking there is one of them to every four or five compositors: and virtually every piece of copy is likely to be checked as well by the sub-editors, the department editor concerned, the person who wrote the story, the editor or the night editor or both, and in many papers, the chief executive, or indeed anyone else around who happens to be interested. At least half-a-dozen people of varying ranks and roles will also check each page for imposition mistakes.

Apart from those concerned with personal safety, it is difficult to think of an industry that pays so much attention to quality: one tends to forget it, but the ultimate quality of composition in at least the final edition of most papers is incredibly near perfection by the normal standards of quality control. Much the same is true of block-making: if one makes the appropriate substitution of photographer for writer and picture editor for department editor, the list above is equally applicable. Print quality is perhaps not so closely watched, mainly because not so many people are interested, but it nonetheless *is* watched: a complaint about print quality is just about the only communication (apart perhaps from lateness) that a management can make with the machine-room during a run. Which is all very good. Except that since, generally, no 'acceptable' levels of quality, other than perfection, have been set, and since quality is as yet subjective and unmeasurable, there are obvious dangers, among them in particular that frustrations resulting from managers' and editors' inability to control other parts of the production process may occasionally boil over into rejection of work that would normally pass. This happens.

Moreover, in anything apart from correcting copy, it is only too often true that such rejection is sporadic and based on an incompetent understanding of the processes in use. I know of one paper where the process department has over the years become used to having occasional blocks criticised on the basis of their appearance in the edition, and to being requested to remake them. They know, and the picture editor knows, that the fault isn't in the blocks, but in the machining; and that moreover it is not so much the fault of the machine-minders as the quality of the machines: when they do make a bad block, they are quick enough to spot it themselves, and remake it without being asked. But the perennial rejections go on, and the department, except occasionally on a hard night, puts up with it with no more than a mild swear word. After all, in spite of all the attention paid to quality control, no one in fact, except a few journalists and managers, ever gets penalised for making mistakes.

The effect all this has on attitudes, and in particular on the respect the unions have for management, is a subject for a later chapter. For the point of this section it is sufficient to record that quality control is still by and large something which management is involved in: indeed it is arguable that it is the sole remaining function of production management.

NEW EQUIPMENT

Another area in which Fleet Street management is given to complaining that it does not have the freedom it should have is over the introduction of new equipment. It is in fact undeniable that the industry has lagged severely behind since the war in introducing the new machinery that has become available, even compared with provincial newspapers in Britain. It is equally undeniable that many machines that have been bought and installed have stayed idle because unions have refused to operate them, from the elaborate and expensive web-offset printing units experimentally installed by the *Daily Mirror* in Belfast for remote production of its Northern Ireland edition (it was finally put permanently out of action by the IRA) to the Klischograph etching machines that have lingered idly around most process departments for varying periods.

Prima facie therefore it would seem that there is ground for asserting that this is another management function which has been usurped by the unions. This however would be objected to by the unions (and, to be fair, many people in management). With legalistic accuracy they point out that they have not been against the introduction of new machinery – in general they welcome it as they would anything that made life easier. What they have stood firm on are the terms on which they will be operated.

Most publishing departments for instance have over the last decade or so introduced mechanised tying and bundling, and in a sense there has been no union resistance to the introduction. Specifically, the unions have simply resisted any suggestion that there should be any loss of income by any of their members as a result, whether from reduced staffing or otherwise. And pretty invariably they have had their way: none of the papers that have mechanised the department have claimed any significant savings from doing so, at least until the normal processes of wastage have had some effect. Most chapels have been open to negotiation, at least a little, on the question of not replacing staff who leave of their own accord.

Much the same is true of the introduction into process departments of automatic block-etching machines, mainly various makes of Klischograph. Nearly all papers have a history of such machines standing around idle while negotiations were pursued about the conditions in which they could be used. At Thomsons the upshot was that two men were required to operate each machine (it is intended for one), and, as is more or less standard throughout Fleet Street, that anyone working on the Klischograph should not do any other work during the night. Since, especially with the earlier models, many prints were unacceptable for etching on the machine, this could mean that after agreements had been concluded, instead of the machine being idle all the time, the machine and two men were idle most of the time. At the *Sunday Times*, introducing two machines led to an increase in the department staff.

Other papers have seen some reduction in process staff as a result. Since the EIU report, though not because of it, on the papers for which I have figures, the number employed has gone down from 339 to 308, nearly 10 per cent, though the situation varies widely from paper to paper, and undoubtedly has something to do with changes in editorial policy and pagination.

In general it appears that Fleet Street managements have not had their power to purchase and install new machinery taken away from them, nor even strenuously fought for. What they have been unable to do is obtain economies to justify the capital cost, though they may have on occasion obtained faster or better quality production. Where the result has been easing the difficulty of the job, or increasing speed or quality, installation has even been welcomed by the unions, once it has been firmly established that no loss of employment or earnings will result.

It is, in passing, a fairly common union complaint, at least within the craft unions, that management has been inadequate in its knowledge of and readiness to introduce new machinery (as well as being reluctant to discuss it openly in advance), but I shall discuss this later, along with other union charges of inadequacy.

EDITORIAL POLICY

In 1972, Mr Wedgwood Benn, as chairman of the Labour Party, gained some extra notoriety for himself by calling on all employed in the communications industries to use their industrial power to ensure that the party's political viewpoint was fairly presented. And it is true that the considerable power of the Fleet Street trade unions, as outlined in the last couple of chapters, could in theory be used to affect, if not control, the editorial content of the newspapers. Indeed, in 1926, it was the refusal of some of the staff of the *Daily Mail* to print an anti-union leader, as recounted in the next chapter, that triggered off the General Strike. But since then at least, the production unions have rarely been tempted to threaten the use of their power to affect the editorial contents of the papers they produce (which is why, presumably, Mr Wedgwood Benn was driven to call on them to do so). They have in fact been much less ready to do anything of the kind than has their counterpart union, the ACTT, (Association of Cinomatograph Television and Allied Techicians) in the television industry.

A few instances of attempted and actual censorship there have admittedly been. They are competently described and discussed in Charles Wintour's book *Pressures on the Press*, but one or two may be worth rehearsing here.

The main thrust of the production unions' attempts to influence content has been to protect the trade union movement in general, and their own interests in particular: and they have not been very active on the first count. Partly this is undoubtedly due to the fact that industrial action for political ends would, except in very rare cases, jeopardise the inter- and intra-union solidarity on which everything else depends: the unions are far from at one in their political stances. But it is probably worth recording here (and discussing again later) the impression I myself have, though I would not claim it as a fact, that, at least among the craft unions there is as much sense of the mission of the Press as there is among journalists, and probably less cynicism about it. It may seem strange, but there undoubtedly exists a fair amount of pride in working for the Press, and working for a free Press: to exercise economic power to damage that freedom is emotionally unacceptable to many. And it is of course also financially unrewarding.

Nonetheless, where it is a matter of protecting their own tactical interests, the situation is somewhat different (as it is for that matter among journalists, editors and proprietors). Then industrial action may be threatened. But there is a great deal of point in writing 'may be' and not 'will be': most of the almost total silence that Fleet Street throws over its own affairs (the troubles NATSOPA had over its May Day strike went unreported, though a lot of space was devoted to other unions' problems in other industries) is, factually, much more the result of a general uneasiness at risking waking sleeping dogs than the consequence of specific threats by the unions.

The position of the NUJ and its members in all this is naturally very different: different enough to postpone it to the chapter on journalists.

SUMMARY

It can hardly be doubted that the degree of control over the production process exercised by management in the newspaper industry is at a level unheard of, let alone acceptable, elsewhere. To produce the paper effectively, if not efficiently, management is dependent on the goodwill, interest in the job, and general inertia of the unions. 'Two things saved British newspapers in the last five years,' one labour specialist told me. 'Decimalisation, which allowed us to put up cover prices without any consumer resistance; and the "blow" system, which means that the unions like the job better than anything else.'

Of all the take-over of managerial functions by the unions, however, the most vital has certainly been the loss by management of any power to influence the individual worker's rewards and punishments, and the subsequent disappearance of any transactional relationship (in an anthropological sense) between the worker and the manager. But that, again, is a topic for later.

7
Union tactics

It would be an exaggeration to claim that the dominance of the unions in Fleet Street has been achieved as the result of a deliberate long-term plan. It is much more the result of a series of successful tactical encounters, coupled with superior ability to react quickly and to learn on one's feet: the campaign of clever guerrillas rather than that of a skilled general. Such tactical superiority is so well established that Fleet Street managements tend to count it as a success if they achieve a stalemate: much as Churchill managed to give Dunkirk the appearance of a victory.

But there are also discernible strategic elements of some significance in union behaviour. Certainly there are more than have been visible on the management side in the past: trouble-shooting and containing the situation is no strategy. At the root of that union strategy, unconscious though it may have been, is concentration on complete control of entry into the trade. On the craft side this is an inheritance from the eighteenth-century, and earlier, apprenticeship system, which, while most craftsmen will admit its illogicality, is still defended by them since it remains a key bastion of their control of the industry.

For the unskilled unions, control over the entry situation is harder. The key dividing line between the craftsman and the NATSOPA or SOGAT worker is that the latter does not serve an apprenticeship, which in effect means only that the union does not control training. (It doesn't mean any less training is required: it may be worth remembering that NATSOPA members include accountants and computer operators as well as messengers and cleaners.) Anyone can learn the jobs that the unskilled unions perform: they therefore lack the inherent strength of the NGA or SLADE (Society of Lithographic Artists, Designers and Engravers).

It is of course also true that anyone can learn to be a journalist: it's even arguable that more of the talent required of a writer or photographer is inborn than learned. Over the last decade or so of increasing militancy among journalists, the NUJ has however set out determinedly to follow the NGA route, with some success. It first of all collaborated willingly with those newspaper managements that set up training schemes for journalists in their affiliated provincial offices (the pattern was established more or less by Kemsley Newspapers). It took part in the formation of NCTJ, the National Council for the Training of Journalists, and the establishment of its three-year (two for graduates) training scheme, which is also based essentially around the provincial newspaper office. At that point I suspect it was probably operating under a reasonably sincere belief that the scheme would contribute to the quality of journalism. (I'm less sure what motivated managements to develop such schemes. It may have only been a desire to emulate more respected industries, but whatever it was they should regret it now.)

However, one result of the Royal Commission of the Press in 1962 was a major change in attitude on the part of the NUJ. In preparing its evidence, and reading other people's, it became evident to the NUJ just how far it and its members had fallen behind vis-à-vis the craft and unskilled unions. And when it began to develop plans to rectify the situation, the NCTJ training scheme was ready as a tool. As a first step, the union began to insist that the national papers recruit only 'qualified' journalists: i.e., existing journalists or recruits who complete the NCTJ apprenticeship scheme. Some papers acceded readily. The *Daily Herald*, as a TUC-sponsored paper, had anyway been an NUJ closed shop for years. The other IPC newspapers, also left-leaning, had also been effective closed shops for a while. But some of the quality papers, notably *The Financial Times* and *The Observer*, were prepared to fight back on the grounds that the NCTJ scheme was on the whole irrelevant to their need for qualified and expert commentators and analysts. Since that argument itself is essentially irrelevant to the NUJ purpose, which is to control the supply of labour to the industry, it is fairly ineffective.

However, for some time a rather uneasy truce has existed, which, as I write, the present government is threatening to break in the union's favour. Expert articles can, at the moment, be commissioned from non-qualified people (i.e., effectively non-NUJ members: non-NUJ journalists are a vanishing breed). And one or two papers are still allowed to continue their previous practice of recruiting university graduates directly as writers, especially on the City pages.

Outside the quality press however the ban on non-NUJ members was complete by the beginning of the 'seventies, even if it had to be politely disguised under the Industrial Relations Act. The union had brought itself up to equality with the craft unions, and quickly put its new strength to use. In the five years, 1968–73, journalists' incomes more than doubled. In achieving control over entry to the profession, it caught up with the craft unions and overtook the unskilled ones. But it still remained (and remains at the time of writing) behind in what has been the second strategic aim of the other unions: to establish and maintain control of the employment exchange. How that operates we saw in the last chapter: its importance from our current point of view is that it makes up for the basic deficiency of the non-craft unions in not having an apprenticeship system. It gives them control over recruitment to the enterprise if not to the industry.

With these commanding heights taken into their control, union strategy is thenceforward dominated by concern for the security of employment and income of their existing members. Whatever may appear in the way of surface demands during negotiations, few if any union officials in Fleet Street are concerned with pay and conditions in the abstract. Their single-minded concern is with ensuring that their present members' life-style is maintained. Thus, for instance, the introduction of labour-saving machinery is resisted if it means lower manning levels, but welcomed if manning levels are maintained, since it reduces effort. The allegedly reactionary unionists are not Luddites from conviction: they are pragmatic enough to prefer an easier life at the same pay.

Alone, these three elements, control of entry to the trade, control of recruitment to the enterprise, and concentration on the interests of specific present members, make up a cohesive strategy that so far has to be matched on the employers' side.

Tactically, too, as I've already said, the unions are undeniably superior. But it isn't only due to their being more capable of thinking quickly or being flexible when flexibility is desirable. Partly it is due to their evolution over the years of a series of tactical ploys. Some of them are subtle, some blunt: and it is to some extent true that the more 'craft' the union, the subtler the technique. Putting them all together, however, one can list them as:

1. *Establishing a moral advantage*
The unions in Fleet Street are on the whole sticklers for agreements. Making agreements legally binding wouldn't help Fleet Street managements much, because by and large the unions keep them to the letter. They are, however, quick to notice, and save for later use as

necessary, management errors or technical breaches of agreements by the management side. Normally, therefore, they are able to go into any dispute in the firm conviction that they are right: which always helps.

Moreover, should they want to introduce change, they are alert to the fact that circumstances alter cases and circumstances are always changing. Many union officials are prepared to admit that the reason they can afford to insist on the letter of agreements is that, if a cause for a new claim is needed, changed circumstances can always be found that invalidate the agreement.

2. *Establishment of superior information*
Unions in Fleet Street frequently claim to know better than management what the commercial position of the company is, day to day. It is difficult to know whether this is true, but in some papers it is undeniably true that the unions, particularly the NGA, keep much more accurate track of output statistics, labour costs, and so on than management does. Partly this is because they deliberately block management attempts to obtain the same information; partly it is because the unions need the information for piece-work distribution, 'fat' payments, casual job allocation, and so on. But it also has to be faced that in most newspapers management has not even tried to collect the kind of work planning and control information that would be routine in most industries. There is no way of knowing if they would succeed if they tried. At least one NGA father of the chapel assures me that he would be quite willing to let management collect the information, but whether that assurance would materialise if put to the test is another matter.

In the meantime, the unions usually have far better detailed information on which to base their claims. And, perhaps more importantly, they are usually able to say, with some conviction, that management is incompetent.

3. *Allegations of conspiracy*
Another tactic that enables the unions to maintain their felt moral superiority is the continuing allegation that management is underhand in the presentation of accounts. Usually the allegation is that newspaper accounts mask profits being made in other parts of the organisation, or through associated companies.

For instance, the chain of deals by which the Thomson Organisation sold *The Times* building to *The Observer* which then sold it to a property company, left the unions involved (at the chapel level anyway) convinced that a massive realisation of property profits was being hidden from them. The conviction strengthened their resolve to make what profit they could from the move of *The Times* to Gray's Inn Road, and disinclined them to pay any attention to appeals based on the loss-making position of the paper itself.

(Their moral indignation was heightened by the belief that the chain of sales was set up to enable the Thomson management to circumvent a trust agreement under which *The Times* building could only be sold to another newspaper.)

4. *Timing the use of opportunities*
This is closely related to some of the things I mentioned under (1), but is not specifically concerned with moral superiority. I have in mind the FoC of a stereotypers' chapel in one paper that was planning a reconstruction of its building. The management went to some lengths to get approval of the planned changes from the unions, but they slipped. They had consulted all the chapels except, for some unknown reason, the stereotypers. In some industries, the shop steward would already have been screaming at the infringement of his status. But Fleet Street unionists take a more pragmatic view. This particular FoC was delighted.

'They've got agreement from the comps,' he said. 'And from the process and the machine-room. From everybody. Except me. And sooner or later they're going to have to come to me. . . .'

The fact that he was in the happy position of being the last to sell outweighed heavily any affront to his dignity.

5. *Exploitation of the short stoppage*
In most manufacturing industries (for that matter in the extractive industries and most agriculture), the output of the production system goes into stock, and deliveries are made from that stock. No matter how simple or how sophisticated the stock control system, the essential principle remains the same: stock functions as a buffer decoupling the production system from the market. Normally, the point of the buffer is to match a steady production flow to a variable sales level. But it can function the other way round. Notably in Scandinavia in recent years stock-holding has facilitated the development of unpaced production systems. And elsewhere stocks provide a safeguard against production fluctuations and stoppages. The

newspaper industry on the other hand does not hold stocks. It cannot, since the essence of a stock system is that the product you make on Tuesday is just as good as the one you make on Wednesday, and you can sell both on Thursday. With very minor and insignificant exceptions, if you don't sell Tuesday's paper on Tuesday, you don't sell it at all.

Newspaper production is therefore directly coupled to the market. In fact, since the disappearance of the sale-or-return system from newspaper retailing, it produces directly to order: a fairly sophisticated and highly accurate system exists for determining each night's print run. The papers as they emerge from the system are already packed, labelled, and addressed to the customer.

As a result, newsapers are immediately vulnerable to a loss of production in a way that no other industry is. Airlines are frequently quoted as a close parallel, since a seat unsold on, say, flight BA753 remains for ever unsold. From a marketing point of view this does provide similarities. But not from the production point of view. If BA753 never flies at all, at least the majority of passengers booked on it will take a later flight – and at least you save the fuel. It tends to be days before an airline strike really starts to turn people to other modes of transport. The longer the distance involved the longer the time lag – travelling to Australia you might as well wait weeks before changing to a ship.

In newspapers generally, however, production lost can neither be made up afterwards nor stockpiled in advance. In the case of the British national newspapers in particular, that situation is worsened by the fact that for most of their circulation they are tightly tied to the times of the newspaper trains from London. A train missed is, effectively, some hundreds of thousands of copies lost, which means not only sales revenue but also advertising income, since advertisers tend to ask for rebates.

This particular vulnerability is one that the unions have learned to exploit. Essentially, there are two methods, short of actually striking (which has the disadvantage from the union point of view that if you strike you don't get paid). One is the calling of chapel meetings at key times during production hours. Considerable subtlety is possible here. Depending on the production schedule of the particular newspaper, a 15-minute meeting at, say, 7, 8 or 10 o'clock may make no difference to production at all. A 15-minute meeting at 9 o'clock on the other hand might mean the loss of the West

Country edition: the same meeting at 11.30 might mean the loss of the commercially much more important Home Counties or Midland and Southern editions.

The alternative to the special meeting is, bluntly, industrial sabotage. The ribbon of fast-flowing and fragile paper on which the rotary printing system is dependent is highly vulnerable. 'Accidents' that tear the web are also remarkably easy to engineer. They take minutes, not hours, to put right: but if those minutes are key ones, thousands, if not tens of thousands, of pounds have been lost – by the company (the workers do not lose anything).

The normally very strong territorial taboos that demarcate the typical newspaper office ensure that the possibility of such 'accidents' is limited to a few chapels (mainly SOGAT and NATSOPA). But the chapel meeting at edition-time is open to all. In particular it has become the chosen weapon of the NUJ in its recent attempts to emulate the success of the other unions.

6. *Use of bluster*

Taboos on improper and immodest behaviour are as strong in newspaper management as in most industrial society. One union father of the chapel I talked to recently happily explained how that worked to his benefit. He'd just told me how a memorandum he'd sent to the production manager on a fairly routine matter hadn't been answered. So far the father of the chapel had taken no notice. 'But,' he said, 'next time I want to see him about something, I go in, and I'm furious. Because I've been ignored. I shout, stamp around, and maybe swear at him. I thump the table a little. And that throws him . . . he's not used to it. Then, when I get to the important point, you know, I'm already winning.'

Such a technique is of course only successful if used sporadically. The key factor is: 'He's not used to it.' But the more successful chapel officials have learned the art of appearing (indeed being) reasonable and properly behaved most of the time, so that the occasional outburst becomes upsetting and frightening.

This is one area in which, as far as I've been able to see, the NUJ has not managed to emulate the other unions, probably because journalists are as trapped by their own behavioural taboos as managers are. For the educated British middle-class, the ability to lose one's temper deliberately, effectively and convincingly is a hard one to acquire. Defensively, most industrial relations specialists in Fleet

Street do tend to develop a protective shell against such outbursts. When you've seen enough of them, tantrums lose their effect. That is one of the reasons which underlie the next and last element in union tactics.

7. *Insistence on going to the top*

Chapel leaders tend to be more or less consciously aware that an important strength in their position is the feeling of inferiority that most newspaper middle managers suffer from, especially vis-à-vis the unions. An important way in which they maintain that feeling is insistence on dealing directly with senior management – and not with 'messenger boys'. Since significant industrial relations decisions in the industry are normally taken by senior management, union insistence on dealing with the bosses directly can be justified rationally. But the emotional aspect is more than just a side effect. Using it to intensify the emotional squeeze on middle management is for many officials a quite deliberate tactic.

One can thus identify seven common tactical policies used to achieve the three main strategic goals. It would be a mistake however to assume that they had emerged as the result of a conscious process of strategic planning. On the contrary they are the result of a long process of evolution in which tactics have been tried out, and, when they succeeded, kept and polished. The fittest have survived, and, as with Darwinian evolution, the result is a process that looks deliberate but isn't.

However, the effect is the same. And it means that the Fleet Street unions will maintain their current superiority until the management side develops a coherent strategy and set of tactics of equal power. Which is something they haven't yet shown any sign of doing.

8

Example – The 8 per cent

In the autumn of 1972, the Conservative government, like the Labour government before it, introduced a short-term standstill on wages. The day before the freeze was due to take effect, the NPA (Newspaper Proprietors' Association) and NATSOPA concluded, rather hastily perhaps, but with no great difficulty, a new wage agreement, which, in general terms gave the union an immediate wage increase of 8 per cent, effective from 1 October, with a further 8 per cent to follow on 1 October 1973.

If the retail price index were to rise by more than 11 points over the September 1972 figure before October 1973, the second half of the rise would take effect immediately: if it rose by more than 22 points before September 1974, the whole agreement would be renegotiated.

Everybody was reasonably happy, except for one thing. The agreement didn't extend to members of the Clerical Branch, who normally negotiate separately, but this time looked liable to be caught by the freeze legislation. That exception led to a situation which provides an illuminating example of Fleet Street negotiations in practice.

To begin with, there was no attempt by the NPA to take advantage of the situation. Some employers, whether wiser or more foolish, might have been tempted to sigh with relief, and say 'hard luck'. But the NPA, whether altruistically or from fear of the consequences or simply out of a sense of fair play, played it differently. There was one apparent loophole. It could be argued that the agreement concluded with the rest of the union had been meant to cover the Clerical Branch, who should therefore be able to benefit under it. The argument sounded reasonable but was not totally convincing. However, one member of the NPA negotiating committee went so far as to telephone the relevant Ministry official to check that it would be o.k.

He confirmed it, and the Clerical Branch negotiators agreed to accept the same terms as the other branches. The terms of the agreement were set out in a letter from the NPA on 4 November 1972. To the NPA and the National Officer conducting the negotiations for NATSOPA, they seemed both clear and acceptable.

Briefly, there would be 8 per cent increases as with the other branches on basic rates and all earnings. Additionally, the NPA pays five increments based on length of service, each of 80p at that time: these were to be increased to £1. And where the 8 per cent and the increased service increments came to less than £2·75 a week, the increase would be made up to that amount. The lowest paid workers would therefore benefit most.

But, then, from Manchester, there came rumblings. The agreement's terms may have been clear, but they were apparently clear in a different way to the members of the Manchester chapels. There is no way of explaining the difference without quoting the text of the letter, at least the relevant part.

Item 2, the 'Monetary Offer', ran:

(*a*) With effect from 1st October 1972, an 8 per cent increase on basic rates and all earnings (including such items as fixed bonuses, etc.). NPA service increments will be adjusted in accordance with clause 2 (*b*) below and will not take the value of the 8 per cent. With effect from 1st October 1973, or as determined by the threshold arrangement as set out in clause 3 below, an increase of 8 per cent on basic rates and all earnings (including such items as fixed bonuses, etc.). NPA service increments will not be adjusted.

(*b*) Each of the five NPA service increments of 80p to be raised on 1st October 1972 to £1. *The 20p increase to be non-absorbable,* and 15p of the 20p to be calculable for overtime.

(*c*) An agreed fall-back of £2·75 per week in the first year to be calculated on the following basis:

> Where 8 per cent and the effect of the amended service increment rates on the average weekly taxable earnings taken over the first 26 weeks of the current tax year yields an increase of less than £2·75 a fixed fall-back payment up to this level will be made.

Section 2 included a futher arrangement for a fall-back of £3 from October 1973, but that is probably enough of that kind of prose for the time being. The snag arose with the sentence I have italicised.

To the NPA the phrase 'non-absorbable' meant that the extra $5 \times 20p$ would not be included in or counted against the 8 per cent increase. A man earning £25 a week would get a £2 increase irrespective of any service increments he might be getting. If he was receiving all five, his weekly pay would therefore go up from £29 to £32. And he would be outside the limits of the £2·75 fall-back clause, which, after all, referred to '8 per cent and the effect of the amended service increment rates'.

The workers in Manchester (to begin with: once the claim was in, some London chapels followed) saw it differently. The 20p increases were to be non-absorbable. And that meant they shouldn't count in calculating the fall-back position. The man above would get £2 for the 8 per cent increase, that would be made up to £2·75, and on top of that he should get the service increments. His eventual pay would therefore be £32·75.

How legitimate that claim is in view of the text is perhaps debatable. Somewhat surprisingly perhaps, even the NATSOPA national officer who had conducted the negotiations supported the NPA view. Even Briginshaw, who came to the NPA to discuss the point, is reported to have been 'lukewarm'. Nevertheless, the Manchester chapels began taking selective action: though, illustrating still further the lack of support for their claim, the machine-room staff went on working.

Perhaps encouraged by that, Frank Rogers, then Director of the NPA, wrote to the union saying that the employers were not prepared to concede the point. (Encouraging him further may well have been the fact that, if the other unions and branches don't support them, you can still get a paper out without the NATSOPA clerks.) Fairly confidently, the NPA expected the NATSOPA national executive to accept the offer – then, as we shall see in Chapter 10, there wouldn't be much the chapels could do. In NATSOPA penalties for disobeying the executive are rather severe.

At the crucial time, however, Briginshaw was away from London. Acceptance or rejection would, in the circumstances, have to await his return. And some people's nerves couldn't stand the strain of waiting. From the unofficial action that had so far taken place, the chief sufferers had so far been the *Sunday Times* (usually liable, for some reason, to take the brunt of NATSOPA action) and the *Daily Telegraph*. Elsewhere the IPC group, Beaverbrook and News International had not 'lost any copies' (i.e., had managed to maintain production completely). But suddenly, these three groups notified the NPA that they were not prepared to stand by the Rogers letter (saying that the employers would not concede). They were prepared to grant the claim.

With the dyke breached, the whole wall had to go. Frank Rogers wrote to the union, reversing his previous position, and conceding the claim. Whether the national executive would have backed the militant action or not remains an open question: it never had to decide.

Ironically, the weekend after the surrender, *The Times* wrote a leader explaining the main points of the situation, justifying it under the terms of the pay freeze – and imploring other employers not to follow the NPA example. To some extent it sounds hypocritical, but to its credit at least *The Times* had been one of the last papers to give in, even though its Sunday sister had been among the worst hit.

As an example, one of the critical points is of course the tangled web of provisions that make up a Fleet Street wage agreement: I didn't quote them, but there is a total of eleven clauses in the agreement quoted here, covering the period of agreement, holidays, weekly hours, inclusive salaries, extra payments for shift and night work, overtime arrangements, adult and junior rates and so on. Craft agreements are usually further complicated by piece-work.

Another is the incredible and legalistic care that has to go into the phrasing of agreements to cover such complexity. And a third is how vain that incredible and legalistic care is, confronted with opponents whose only concern is how to break it.

But the major observation that needs to be made is of the weakness typically displayed by the NPA. If nothing else has been in the last five or ten years, this was an issue on which it looked quite possible to fight. The union's claim was unofficial, and not very convincing. As far as anyone can tell, it didn't have, and wasn't likely to get, national support. Even the machine branches on the same papers weren't prepared to support it. And the group making the claim were potentially one of the weakest in the industry, at least in terms of their power to disrupt production.

But still the employers gave in. Without playing a card.

9
The craft unions

The origins of the craft unions in the British printing industry go back deep into history. But the same is true in other countries: this fact by itself would not be important except that in its structure and its rules and regulations, the British union structure is not only ancient, it is also antique. In other words, to the outsider at least, the system has characteristics that do not fit current circumstances – characteristics that are indeed harmful to any attempt to make the organisation and technology of the industry match the demands being made on it in the modern world, and to do so rationally and economically.

One obvious instance has already been mentioned: the apprenticeship system which is common to all the crafts but for which we might as well take the compositors' example as a paradigm. Before he can be employed on a British newspaper, the compositor has to have served a six-year apprenticeship. What is more, that apprenticeship must have been served in the 'general trade' – i.e. outside newspapers. Apprentice entry (throughout the printing industry) is strictly controlled by the union both in terms of numbers and of selection, and in Fleet Street in particular that control is exercised to prevent effectively the use of apprentices at all.

Newspaper managements are therefore prevented from hiring trainee compositors. All they can do is engage fully-trained men who have spent six years and more learning skills the majority of which have no utility in, or even relevance to, the national newspaper industry.

Historically, the practice goes back to the Elizabethan Statute of Artificers, which made the seven-year apprenticeship compulsory for all crafts. It was repealed in 1817, so that for most industries it has nothing but antiquarian interest. But by 1817 the compositors, at least in London, were already more or less successfully organised on a trades union basis, and had indeed already fought their first (largely successful) strike action. And for a quarter of a century before that, limitation of apprenticeships had been as important a goal as the increase of wages and piece-rates.

In 1786, strike action had been threatened against John Walter I, founder of *The Times*, for employing an extra apprentice in his book-printing house. Under the threat of prosecution for combination, the strike never took place and Walter continued to recruit more apprentices in what he was later to admit was a deliberate campaign to weaken the position of the journeymen he employed. In that he was helped by being able to advertise in his own paper, but it is worth noting that when he tried to advertise for boys in *The Daily Advertiser*, its proprietors, under pressure from their own journeymen, refused to accept the advertisement and returned his money. It may also be worth noting that the notice issued on that occasion was signed by William Larman, as secretary of the 'General Meeting of the Trade', on behalf of the 'delegates': the earliest recorded evidence of the existence of a formally constituted trade society in the industry.

The campaign for control over apprentice entry was waged throughout the nineteenth century and not finally won until the twentieth. But the premiss behind it remained constant: the over-riding importance of controlling the supply of a commodity if you want to control its price. To attain that object of course it is not enough simply to be able to dictate the number of apprentices taken on. It is equally essential to maintain the craft status of the job: to ensure that only men who have served their time are employed. Under the Statute of Apprentices that goal was not difficult, though there were occasional disputes with the master printers during the eighteenth century, particularly over the employment of unapprenticed labour as fly hands. Employers were usually ready to back down under the threat of prosecution under the Statute. The repeal of the Statute however coincided with the arrival of the steam press, a reactionary political climate, and a difficult to explain lull in organised activity among newspaper workers. (There are no records of such activity in London from 1820 to 1833.) As a result, some concessions were made. In the composing-room, non-craft workers were allowed to take proofs. In the machine-room, the only job that continued to require a craftsman was that of supervising the machine – the machine manager as he was beginning to be called. Other ancillary jobs (including the once-vexed position of fly hand) were allowed to be performed by unskilled labour.

But the movement stopped there. Resurgence of organised activity in the 'thirties ensured that the demarcation line between craft and non-craft was held, and with one or two minor exceptions (of more importance in the next chapter) the lines remain the same at the present day. The last major battle was probably that fought in 1852, when the *Morning Post* and *The Sun* attempted to break the monopoly of the London craftsmen by importing labour from Scotland. A well-organised defence committee defeated the attempt through the mass distribution of pamphlets and posters, by persuading licensed victuallers and coffee-houses not to take the two papers, and with the collaboration of some of the other craft unions employed by the papers, notably the bricklayers and the carpenters and joiners.

Even the arrival of composing machines, later in the century, failed to disturb the situation. Notably, the machine-room solution, skilled minder and unskilled assistants, was never introduced, and as a result early machines like the Hattersley which were only economic when unskilled labour could be used to redistribute type never gained a place in newspaper composing-rooms (apart from semi-experimental installation at *The Times*). Not until the arrival of the Linotype, which required no assistants, did machine composition become part of newspaper production. The weaknesses of 1815–35 were never allowed to occur again.

Indeed, as far as the other two major crafts of newspaper production were concerned, these weaknesses never happened at all. Neither stereotyping nor process blocks were part of newspaper production till the latter half of the century, when the importance of organisation and the maintenance of craft distinction were both well recognised. As a result these remain the most exclusive of the production crafts. By analogy with the composing-room, some process departments allowed unskilled labour to be used in taking proofs. But no work inside the foundry is allowed to be performed by unskilled men (even cleaning and sweeping): for a non-craftsman even to walk through the department tends to heighten tension.

In a chapter overtly dedicated to present-day attitudes, such a historical digression may seem out of place. But without an understanding of the historical background it is impossible to arrive at any understanding of the present position of the newspaper craftsman. It would be an exaggeration to say that Fleet Street craftsmen are all knowledgeable historians (though a surprising number are) but the sense of historical continuity is strong, and by and large the attitudes and self-image of the craftsman are still those of his predecessors of a century and more ago. Notably, for instance, the craftsman's self-image is not that of an employee. His view of the relationship with the newspaper management is still that of the independent journeyman hiring out his services (via his union) on equal terms. Psychologically, if not legally, he works the 'lump'. It may be only symbolic, but it is nonetheless true, that the pay of most compositors is determined not by a 'wage agreement', but by the 'London Scale of Prices'.

Once one realises that fundamental truth, and stops trying to see the compositor, and the craftsman in general, as an employee in the way that word is used in most industries, then some of the more puzzling aspects of Fleet Street management become easier to understand. Attempt to impose an orthodox organisation structure on the *Daily Mirror* for instance, and you end up with something over nine hundred people reporting to the machine-room manager, a span of control to confuse the textbooks. View those nine hundred people as 'outside' labour, engaged by and working through the union (two unions to be accurate) as a contractual supplier, and the situation begins to make more sense.

Other things fall into place too. The fact that take-home pay is determined by the father of the chapel, through his control over the allocation of such things as fat and overtime; the fact that individuals are free to work more or less what hours they like as long as it is acceptable to their workmates; the fact that payments are made by management on the basis of notional manning standards rather than actual manning; the fact that hiring and firing and discipline in general are matters for the union, not for management; all these become natural elements of the pattern given the understanding that the management contracts with the union for the performance of certain tasks, and the employer/employee relationship exists only on paper. And that understanding follows from the realisation that the present craft unions are in direct line of historical continuity from the medieval guilds.

Other things also follow from that historical continuity. In the medieval and early modern periods for instance, the guild member could rely on the assistance of his association if he should fall on hard times. And with barely a break that role has continued to be played by the craft unions. For sustenance while sick or unemployed, for benefits on retirement, even, during the period of imperial expansion, for assistance with emigration, the print craftsman has automatically been able to look to his union for well over a century (the last of these benefits to be introduced, for retirement, was introduced in 1874, though the first payments, of 5 to 10 shillings per week, were not made until 1877).

Loyalty to the union is therefore deeply ingrained: this loyalty is not based on ideology or class solidarity but on the much more pragmatic foundation of mutual benefit. 'My union, right or wrong', is not a cry that most Fleet Street craftsmen would want, or feel bound, to follow: 'my union, while it's working for me', would match the general attitude better. While most union members may vote Labour, and most union officials may be members of the Labour party, the essential mood of the craft unions is therefore bourgeois: Marx and Engels would have shaken their heads at it just as much as left-wing socialists still do today.

Some of the early pronouncements of the craft unions sound indeed not only bourgeois but priggish: 'The fault of the Trades Unions has hitherto been that they have copied the vices which they professed to condemn. While disunited and powerless they have stigmatised their employers as grasping taskmasters; but as soon as they were united and powerful then they became tyrants in their turn, and unreasonably endeavoured to exact more than the nature of their employment demanded, or more than their employers could afford to give . . . Let the compositors of London show the artisans of England a brighter and better example; and casting away the aid to be derived from cunning and brute strength, let us, when we contend with our opponents, employ only the irresistible weapons of truth and reason.'

And: '. . . have we not a right to expect that the compositors of London, from their superior station in the rank of artisans, have learnt that they can never better themselves by the exaction of higher wages than the profits of capital can allow; but that they nevertheless have a right, as a body, to regulate their numbers as in some degree to proportion the supply of labour to the demand, and if possible secure to each member of the trade such a quantity of employment as shall prevent him from being a mendicant dependant on the classes above him.'

No present-day Fleet Street craftsman is going to talk about 'the classes above him', any more than he is likely to wallow in the same degree of Victorian humbug. But his essential attitudes have barely changed. What counts is not ideology or doctrine but securing 'to

each member of the trade' a secure livelihood 'as great as the profits
of capital will allow' and befitting his 'superior station in the rank
of artisans'.

Something of the same attitude was even manifest in the 1926
General Strike. The printing unions were among those in the 'front
line' of unions called on by the TUC to strike from midnight on
3 May. On 1 May, a Saturday, the Joint Board of the London
Society of Compositors met to consider the call: the minutes of its
meeting record: 'The circular from the General Council was considered, and the Secretary instructed to reply that we should have
to consult our members before we could co-operate in the General
Strike suggestion.'

On the day before the strike was due to begin, the Board met
again and passed a resolution deploring the TUC policy, but it did
manage to find a way out, resolving: 'That owing to the untenable
position created by the cessation of all the vital industries, including
the means of getting to and from work, this Committee has no
alternative but to advise the delegate meeting to agree to a general
cessation of work.'

Not precisely the dedication to the workers' cause that Ernest
Bevin, say, might have wanted to see: nor on the whole was any
such dedication evidenced by the National Graphical Association
in the years of opposition to the Conservative Government's
Industrial Relations Act. The NGA, preferring the security of its
assets and its preferential tax position to ideology, registered under
the Act, thereby incurring expulsion from the TUC. But its attitude
was perhaps best symbolised by the reaction to the TUC's call for a
one-day strike on 1 May 1973 against the Act.

NATSOPA and SOGAT, the unskilled unions, responded satisfactorily
(and not surprisingly, as we will see in the next chapter). So too,
initially did the NGA's National Executive. But the executive of the
NGA cannot call a strike without a ballot; and it was outvoted by
the chapels, who decided to work. Or rather, for this is the heart
of the story, not to work, but to get paid. One father of the chapel,
off-duty a solid enough Labour party member, put it succinctly
enough to me: 'With NATSOPA out, the papers won't publish anyway,
so what difference does it make what we do? If we strike, we don't
work and we don't get paid. If we don't strike, we don't work,
and we get paid. And either way I'll be joining in the protest
march.'

John Bonfield, then General Secretary of the NGA, shows a similar pragmatism when he says: 'I'm a Socialist, I believe in a Socialist world, and I'll work to create one. But in the meantime, we live in a capitalist world, a jungle. And while that's true, we'll play the capitalist game.'

Playing the capitalist game implies concentrating on material benefits, including job security, for present members. And that pragmatic preoccupation has resulted in the evolution of the craft unions as highly democratic organisations. As the General Strike memorandum implied and the May Day strike refusal indicated, political strength within the craft unions lies overwhelmingly with the local chapels, which are free in effect as well as on paper to settle their own affairs in their own way.

The matter of registration under the Industrial Relations Act was another case in point. The National Executive, more conscious of wider political issues, was in favour of the TUC ban on registration, and recommended to the membership that the union should not register. But it was overwhelmingly defeated by voting at the chapel level, where the practical benefits of registration outweighed any considerations of party political strategy. (There was as a result some bitterness in the craft unions at the Labour government's proposals in 1974 to compensate financially those unions that did not register. This was not based on any right-wing feeling that other unions were wrong not to obey the law: the craft unions are as ready as anyone to ignore the law if it is to their advantage to do so. Rather it is a feeling that refusal to register was a foolish piece of flag-waving, that it had no important effect on the eventual outcome, and that if the mass of unions had followed the NGA path, they could have saved their money and still had the Act repealed. In craft union philosophy, if you can have your cake and eat it, then you should.)

Preoccupation with material benefit at the expense of wider issues, especially in a group which on the whole is better educated and more intelligent than the average tends to produce a dissonance between formal, outward behaviour and informal conversation that I suppose can only be identified as cynicism. At least it breeds cynical modes of speech.

Thus, formally, the craft unions still insist on the maintenance of craft standards, with all this implies in the matter of training. They are still preoccupied with preventing what one stereotyper

FoC christens 'the March of the Nats' (Nat= member of NATSOPA). Yet privately any member of the craft unions will readily admit that the level of skill demanded of craft operatives in any job in the modern newspaper is minimal – is indeed far below the level that most have been trained to reach during their apprenticeship and work in the general printing trade. In their study in 1966, the Economist Intelligence Unit calculated that the most time required for learning any of the craft jobs they observed was one year (for Linotype composition, and to reach the average level of proficiency, not just to learn to operate the machine). I haven't found anyone in the craft unions to disagree with that assessment, and I doubt that anyone would – informally.

However, while it is obvious to the craftsman that they are over-trained, it is equally obvious that were the craft barriers to recruitment to be lifted, then their personal positions would be weakened. That was the lesson the unions learnt in the 1830s, it is still true, and it hasn't been forgotten. Both tactically and strategically therefore it becomes imperative for the craft unions to maintain inter-job status differentials.

Sometimes the dissonance reaches curious heights. As individuals, many union members and officials are prepared to admit the irrationality of craft distinctions in, say, the machine-room, and to accept the logical attraction of joint training schemes specifically for the newspaper industry, abandoning the link with the general trade. I once met an NGA FoC who in fact had spent a considerable amount of his own time and effort in designing such a scheme, on a modular basis, with different entry points and choice points in moving through it, and including the possibility of adding in university education where desirable. Effectively the scheme could produce, as members of a single industry union, everything from assistants and craftsmen to journalists and managers, and one can imagine many personnel managers falling on it with glee. (Though it is worth noting that it represents a recrudescence of the medieval guild system in that it assumes the individual committing himself to a vocation in his teens, and would rule out mature entry from outside.) But he had no intention of ever advocating its introduction. Not only because of its political unacceptability to others, but because he himself is probably doing better under the present scheme.

It is difficult to see therefore that management arguments for such things as the elimination of craft demarcation or the abolition of the apprenticeship system are ever going to get very far. Normally they are based on intellectual, logical arguments – the kind of argument that the Economist Intelligence Unit produced. But at that level there is no need for argument since the case is already won: craft workers are prepared to admit, are indeed themselves convinced, of the illogicality and inefficiency of the present situation. But it works in their favour, as a group and as individuals, and it will therefore take a very different kind of argument to induce them to welcome any change: namely, an argument that says 'this way you will be more secure and make more money'. It isn't easy to see how such an argument can carry conviction.

A similar pattern is evident in craft attitudes to the introduction of new machinery (and for that matter of new management techniques). At an intellectual level, interest among craftsmen in new equipment and new methods is high. Indeed there is a general feeling, which has some justification, among many FoCs at least that they know far more about the potential benefits of new technology than management does. They are even eager to try out and use new equipment, not only because it is usually effort-saving, but also from sheer vocational interest – the attitude is much that of the hi-fi enthusiast talking of new and expensive equipment he hasn't yet been able to afford. And the key phrase there is 'able to afford'. From the craftsman's point of view, new equipment, however desirable, which threatens jobs or earnings cannot be afforded: he therefore denies himself it, at least until he has sufficient guarantees to remove the threat.

It took years to introduce, for instance, Klischograph engraving machines into Fleet Street process departments, and when they were introduced they weren't from a management point of view all that economic since they had to be overmanned. Tactically, in the negotiations, the unions made much of the machine's inadequacy and lack of quality. Once installed however such arguments were forgotten: within a very short time every picture that could be handled by the machine was being sent to it rather than being processed by hand. The machine was highly acceptable, but only when it posed no threat.

Union disparagement of management's knowledge of technical affairs is paralleled by cynicism about the level of skill required and displayed by management (and journalists) in general. At a general level one cannot help liking the (Groucho) Marxist implications of 'If they were any good they wouldn't let us get away with what we do', a view fairly commonly expressed.

Management generally is seen as being spineless, easy to browbeat, shortsighted, and incohesive (as between different newspapers). The break away from the NPA of the IPC newspapers was seen of course as further evidence of such disunity – encouragingly since it presages continuance of the dominance of the unions, discouragingly in that the commonest reason given by the unions for the weakness of the industry is internecine strife between managements.

It is a matter of record that the unions were pressing managements to increase cover prices long before the price escalation of the later 'sixties and 'seventies began: the incident is still used as evidence of the superior understanding of the unions of the realities of the economic situation. Union officials are also ready to assume that the weakness in bargaining skills which is generally evident to them at first hand is carried over from the labour relations situation to the commercial one. One instance quoted to me several times was the industry's reaction (or lack of reaction) to the ban on cigarette advertising on television. From the pragmatic point of view of the craft unions it is impossible to understand why publishers did not automatically respond by charging a stiff premium for the same advertising in newspapers and magazines.

One FoC, a compositor, to make his point that anyone could sell space, some years ago got himself a job as a newspaper space salesman. I have no evidence of his claims to have outsold his predecessor within a couple of weeks: but the important point is that the experience did nothing to alter his or his colleagues' view that, no matter how easy the work they themselves do, everything on the commercial side is easier still. As someone else put it: 'To work as a comp or a machine-minder you've got to serve your apprenticeship . . . you've got to prove you're good at something even if it isn't very relevant to what you actually do. But to be a manager in Fleet Street you don't have to be good at anything.' Whether that is true or not is really beside the point. The important thing is that it leaves the average craft union member confident of his own superiority (or that of his representatives) over management – in particular at the negotiating table. And it adds a final touch to the general picture of the Fleet Street craft unions as a self-confident and self-assured group of men who are over-trained, over-educated and over-intelligent for the jobs they have to do: a surplus of ability that they can afford to dedicate to their primary task of maximising their own well-being.

For anyone concerned with the long-term health of the industry there are perhaps only two gleams of hope. One is that on the whole the craft unions are too intelligent to cut their own throats. And the other is that their disregard of broader issues includes a disregard for generations of craftsmen to come. There is no dedication to the craft cause, simply a dedication to the craftsman currently employed in the industry. A long-term plan (should anyone in the industry ever begin to think that far ahead) to sort out what is generally agreed to be an inefficient mess may have some chance of success as long as it contains sufficient guarantees not to threaten the present comfort of the present craftsmen.

10

Unskilled unions

It is an insult to any body of men to be asked to agree to remain
at the bottom of the ladder all their lifetime, and to be 'instructed'
to refuse all offers of promotion is more than human nature can
stand, especially when we are of the opinion that our members
have a prior claim to promotion to take charge of rotary letterpress
machines over any and every other class of workmen. We have
to begin at the bottom and by merit alone, our members are
promoted by stages to more responsible positions, and finally are
to be barred, by a line drawn in favour of persons who have not
one quarter of the knowledge possessed by our members of this
class of machine.

That passage was written as long ago as 1912 by George Isaacs,
when general secretary of NATSOPA; yet it contains the marrow of
what is still the major bone of contention, at least overtly, between
the two halves of the trade union movement in Fleet Street, the
'skilled' and the 'unskilled'. As I described in the last chapter, in
the period of union weakness that followed Waterloo, unskilled
(i.e. unapprenticed labour) was allowed into newspaper printing
houses in various ancillary jobs: by the 1830s however the unions
had regained enough strength to ensure that, in general, the
principle that the man in charge of a press should be a craftsman was
strictly followed.

It was still true in 1912, and it is still true today. A man who starts
work as an assistant on a rotary press can be promoted through
various grades until he becomes a 'brake hand'. But there he stops:
since he has no apprenticeship qualification he can never become
a machine manager. On the other hand, an NGA member who has
the necessary six-year apprenticeship plus two as a journeyman
can be appointed to the job, even if he has never seen a rotary press
in his life.

That such a system should create resentment and frustration is of
course inevitable. It is however a little more surprising that the
consequent emotional reaction should be so widespread through the

entire union, in view of the fact that only a minority of its members are actually employed in the machine-room, and that elsewhere in the industry the demarcation is nothing like so flagrant.

As I've pointed out, in some departments it doesn't exist at all. In the foundry, all employees are craftsmen. In the photographic darkroom all workers are NATSOPA, skilled or unskilled. In the composing-room and the process department, it exists, but has some objective rationale in that the jobs done by the NGA and SLADE at least require a different training from those done by NATSOPA. In the reading-room, while the same demarcation exists as in the machine-room (all readers are NGA, their assistants are NATSOPA), there are no barriers to promotion from one grade to the other – indeed most readers start out as assistants. And in addition, all the union's white-collar workers are members of NATSOPA: outside the production departments, demarcation does not exist.

For the majority of the union membership, the machine-room situation can therefore be no more than a symbol: but it is a symbol with a powerful emotional appeal, and one that over several years has involved the whole union in industrial action.

In the official history of NATSOPA, James Moran politely made a point that is frequently made by NATSOPA members with rather less consideration for propriety. He wrote:

> We may laugh now at the attempts of the eighteenth-century Tallow Chandlers to keep gas lighting from the streets of London as being harmful to their trade . . . But in seeking to protect particular crafts certain unions have, in effect, been seeking also for a permanently stratified society, which seems at odds with egalitarian views expressed at other times.

NATSOPA therefore sees the craft unions as hypocritical in their overt socialist allegiance, and dedicated to the preservation of an unfair society: as I wrote in the last chapter, the craft unions are essentially bourgeois in their motivation and their behaviour. In contrast, NATSOPA is frequently politically or ideologically motivated and will (in craft union terms) 'cut off its nose to spite its face' to make a political point. Which, of course, is what it did in striking against the Industrial Relations Act.

The machine-room situation, whatever its symbolic value, is not enough to explain that ideological clash. To arrive at a fuller understanding, as in the last chapter, it is necessary to look at the historical background – though there is no need to go quite so far back this time.

The origins of the craft unions lie in the medieval guilds and the Elizabethan Statutes of Apprentices: the origins of the unskilled unions, both NATSOPA and SOGAT, lie however in the wave of working-class militancy that swept over England in the 1880s. This was the decade when, throughout British industry, the labouring proletariat (as opposed to the artisans) first began to organise themselves and to exercise the power that organisation gave them. It was the time of some of the best-remembered early strikes, still capable of arousing emotional responses in the modern movement: the match-girls' strike of 1888 and the London dockers' in 1889. It also included the year (1887) in which the Social Democratic Federation, after failing to make any headway in orthodox politics, officially decided that its members should turn their attention to working through trade union organisation – the beginning of the somewhat sporadic attachment of British labour to socialism.

And it was at the very end of the decade, in August 1889, that the unskilled printing workers of London organised their first strike. Their key demand was for a wage of £1 for a 54-hour week, plus 6d an hour overtime, itself an indication of a change of attitude from that of the craft printers, whose major preoccupation was always with piece-work rates (the London Scale of Prices). Equally indicative of a change of felt allegiance was their adoption of the paraphernalia of the mass unions: bands, processions, banners emphasised their link with the other labouring unions, and distinguished them from the rather more discreet and 'professional' craftsmen. A frequent speaker at their meetings was the propagandist Mrs Annie Besant who had provided both the finance and the inspiration for the match-girls' strike the year before.

Effectively, the strike was very quickly successful, although a handful of printing houses held out for some months. But more important than the strike itself was the fact that out of it grew the first permanent unskilled union in the industry: the Printers' Labourers' Union. Ironically, its first General Secretary, one George Evans, was himself a craftsman, a compositor, who was also already an active social democratic propagandist. In fact, having established the union, he resigned as secretary the following year, and subsequently rather vanished from sight. In the annals of NATSOPA (the name 'Printers' Labourers' Union' was changed in 1899) Evans still has an

E

honoured place: in the official history of the London Society of Compositors, however, he goes unmentioned.

The union was thus born in highly class-conscious and politically dominated circumstances: and it has subsequently remained the most politically committed of the Fleet Street unions. The true events of the week-end of 1/2 May 1926 are more than a little difficult to uncover: but it seems fairly well established that whatever chance there was to stave off the General Strike which had been called for the following week was destroyed on the Sunday, when workers on the *Daily Mail* refused to print an article they considered unfair on the union position. When the government heard the news, it broke off negotiations, and the strike was on.

Officially, NATSOPA through George Isaacs, the General Secretary, disowned the strikers' action, and subsequently the union has always been at pains to point out that members of other unions were involved. But it remains undeniable that the strikers' spokesman was a NATSOPA official, and highly probable that the action started with the NATSOPA chapel. And given the dictatorial powers of NATSOPA's central organisation (of which more later), it seems incredible that Isaacs (who was on the spot during the evening) couldn't have called off the action if he had wanted.

The action certainly contrasts strongly with the compositors' lukewarm acceptance of the strike call which I recorded earlier.

Isaacs himself, a Labour MP off and on from 1924 onwards, and an under-secretary in the Ramsay McDonald government of 1929–30, provides an excellent symbolic example of the close relationship which NATSOPA has had with party and national politics. From 1945–48 he was at the same time Minister of Labour under Attlee and General Secretary of the Union: a somewhat rare blend of interest. (Herbert Morrison, when first elected to Parliament, was also a member of NATSOPA, though he was never prominent in its internal affairs.)

Under Isaacs, perhaps not surprisingly, the union fairly staunchly followed the official Labour party line. Under Richard Briginshaw, who was first elected secretary in 1951, it has shifted sharply to the left, but lost none of its interest in political matters. Since the 'fifties it has generally aligned itself with that section of the party that has advocated disarmament, opposed German rearmament and Common Market membership for Britain, fought for the retention of 'Clause IV' in the Labour party's constitution, and generally taken a predictable line on matters that the Fleet Street craft unions would consider of no relevance to the unions' tasks.

It is an interesting sidelight on another distinction between the craft unions and NATSOPA that it is perfectly possible to write of the history of the craft unions without mentioning any individuals by name. It is impossible to do the same with NATSOPA. From its very beginning, it has been effectively dominated by a series of 'strong men', of whom Briginshaw is merely the latest. In its first 85 years of existence, it has had only seven general secretaries, most of whom held office in the first decade:

George Evans (1889–90)
Thomas O'Grady (1890–7)
Michael Vaughan (1897–8)
Edwin Smith (1899–1909)
George Isaacs (1909–48)
Harry Good (1948–51)
Richard W. Briginshaw (1951–time of writing)

The first of them, I have already mentioned. The next two were both ultimately dismissed for neglect of their duties (though, as far as one can see, O'Grady in particular did a great deal to put the union on a well-organised footing). From the records, what does seem likely is that neither of them was very capable of handling members of a union which, according to its own official history, suffered from 'an addiction to fisticuffs'. The same could not be said of Edwin Smith, who was popularly known to members as 'Mighty Smith'. Smith it was who had the name of the union changed to 'Operative Printers' Assistants' Society' (because some of the men they were recruiting in newspaper machine-rooms objected to being called 'labourers'), who extended its activities to the provinces, established the power of the executive committee to negotiate and settle terms, bought the freehold of Caxton House, still NATSOPA's headquarters, and brought women members into the union (in a section organised by his sister, Miss E. M. R. Smith). Unfortunately, it was also Smith who, in the words of the official history, got the unions funds 'into a state of confusion with those of a sick benefit society with which he was connected', and retired rather hastily to Canada, leaving the Society with funds of 3/3d, mortgages on its property, and sundry liabilities of £1,100.

Smith's sister was sacked (and the post of female organiser abolished), the Society's accountants were changed, and a settlement made with the receiver who was now looking after the 'One and All Sickness & Accident Corporation', regarding a loan from the Corporation to the Society which had been partially repaid, though by different amounts in the two sets of books. No accusations of fraudulent behaviour were ever made against Smith, who came back to England for a visit in 1925 and was warmly received by the union, the London Branch in particular. Isaacs wrote him a friendly letter: 'Hoping that our forgetfulness of disagreements and recollections of good service may be mutual, and that you will accept this communication in the spirit in which it is sent. . . .' Smith wrote back: 'You may rest content that whatever doubt I had of the members' belief in my sincerity and integrity is now vanished from my mind forever. . . .'

That was sixteen years later however. In the meantime Isaacs had taken over, and become firmly established in the position he was to hold for all but forty years. Up until 1908 he had held no official position in the union, though he had tried vainly for election to the Executive Committee in 1907 and 1908. Then he was appointed chairman of a small committee set up to investigate the Society's financial affairs: and on the retirement of Smith was asked to take over as General Secretary *pro tem*. In October 1909 the appointment was confirmed by ballot.

Within three years he had transformed the Society's shaky finances, opened a series of new provincial branches and successfully organised the Society's share of the general printing strike of 1911 (the 'hours' strike which was fought for a 50-hour week, and which, *inter alia*, saw the launch of the *Daily Herald* as the unions' own paper). He had also had the name of the union changed again: it was now the 'National Society of Operative Printers & Assistants'. The significance lies in the '&', which replaced the previous apostrophe. From this point on the union was to lay at least titular claim to representing printers in general, not just their assistants. For the craft unions, the 'March of the Nats' had started.

It was still some years, however, before Isaacs' own control over the union was to be fully established. He had won one battle in 1911, when the national organiser, James Norey, was sacked by the Executive Committee for incompetence and 'attacking the general secretary'. But from 1920–22 he had to fight a further series of battles (though helped now by the fact that he had established the *Natsopa Journal* under his own editorship). The opposition to

Isaacs was mainly London-based, led by an organisation which called itself the 'United Chapels' and objected on a string of issues which included the way in which the union's finances were conducted, the political activities of some of its officers, the way in which ballots were conducted, and the General Secretary's control of the *Journal* and the meetings of the Governing Council. The prime mover of the opposition appears to have been Edwin Smith's brother, a machine-room assistant on the *Daily Mirror*.

Isaacs however made full use of a tactic which is familiar enough in other circles. In 1920, under attack from some quarters for the money he had spent on the creation of a Memorial Home (containing a sanatorium, a convalescent home, and cottages for aged members), he resigned. The Executive came to heel at once, and among other things gave him three months' leave in America – he had already been in close contact with the International Printing Pressmen and Assistants of North America, and had paid two visits to them, one before and one during the war. In 1922, at the height of the pressure from the United Chapels, he repeated the tactic. He asked the Executive Council to declare the general secretaryship vacant, stating specifically that the action was to be taken to enable members to express their confidence or otherwise in the way he had been carrying out his duties. He was re-nominated, obviously, and there were three other nominations, named Dunn, Rumsey, and Siequien. An examining board was appointed by the council to 'put the candidates for the general secretaryship to the test'. It consisted of seven members of the Executive Council, and 'the General Secretary was to attend in his official capacity'. It may not be too surprising that the examining board reported:

> Messrs Dunn, Rumsey and Siequien have not satisfied us of their fitness and suitability for the duties involved. We further record the opinion that each of the individuals named are inefficient and totally unsuitable and unfit for the duties of the post for which they are candidates.

Actually, the Executive Council decided nevertheless to let their names go forward on to the ballot paper. But the three 'unfit' candidates, perhaps predictably, insisted their names were withdrawn: they even took legal action to have the ballot declared void, on the grounds that their names ought not to have been inserted as they had been found unfit for the post.

Eventually, Isaacs was elected unopposed. From then on, he and the union were effectively one.

As indeed has been the case with the union and its present General Secretary, Richard Briginshaw, since his election in 1951. (Harry Good, who was elected in 1948 to succeed Isaacs when he reached retirement age, had an accident in 1950 and had to retire through illness the following year. He was a Scotsman who had been district secretary in the North-Eastern Division: Briginshaw, like Isaacs and Smith, was a London machine-room man.)

In achieving that solidarity, both Briginshaw and Isaacs were aided by a rule-book that contrasts markedly with the democratic (not to say anarchic) organisation of the NGA. Officially, the sovereign body in the union is the Governing Council, elected on the basis of one delegate for every 500 members. But the Governing Council meets only once a year, in normal circumstances anyway: effective power lies with the Executive Council. And its power *is* effective. To begin with, it has power to call any members of the union out on strike, or to order them to take any other industrial action whatsoever. Equally, it has power to refuse to recognise any action taken by the chapels or branches: in which case it can expel from the union anyone continuing with such action. In general, it can fine or expel any member for a variety of reasons including, in blanket fashion, 'acting contrary to rules or in a manner detrimental to the Society's welfare'. Moreover, it can bar from holding office in the union anyone who, *in its opinion*, is guilty of conduct proving him not to be 'a fit and proper person to hold office'. That includes elected office. Indeed, the practice adopted in the election for General Secretary of 1922, having the Executive Council appoint an examining board to report on the fitness of all nominated candidates for office, is still enshrined in the rule-book.

There is more to it than that. Membership of the Executive Council is not proportional to general membership in the way that of the Governing Council is. Instead there is specific provision that it should consist of four members from the London Machine Branch, two from the London 'Revisers and General Assistants' (i.e. the rest of the London production workers), three from the clerical branches nationally, two from Manchester and the South-East, and one each from all other districts. Effectively therefore the council is dominated by the London membership, particularly the Machine Branch: especially since the quorum for meetings is seven, and all meetings take place in London. The domination is magnified by the fact that the London members can meet as an emergency committee, in which case they have the full powers of the Executive Council – as long as five members are present.

Such meetings can be called by the General Secretary, through whom all Executive Council and Governing Council business must anyway be submitted. A General Secretary who is in close collaboration with the delegates of the London Production branches therefore in practice controls the union (including controlling the nominations for elective office).

Such a situation would be unacceptable to the craft unions, but is not untypical of mass movements. Equally the craft unions would be unlikely to accept the NATSOPA Executive Council's specific power to order any action 'to assist the members of other Trade Unions or their Branches in any strike or lockout or trade dispute or movement' and 'to support and advance generally Trade Union principles, customs and usages'. This sense of formal solidarity with other unions is reflected in the rule that makes it an offence punishable by fine or expulsion to work for any employer if any of his other workers are on strike, whether or not they are members of NATSOPA.

Not that this has prevented NATSOPA members working when other union members have been on strike, as when the NUJ struck against United Press International in 1972, and lost because of lack of support from any other unions.

In view of the overt political stance taken by NATSOPA, and the way in which its structure ensures that it acts as a political unit, one of the charges launched by the craft unions through the 'sixties may seem a little odd. This was that NATSOPA and management were collaborating to the detriment of the craft position.

How much actual truth there is in that suggestion I don't know: but it is not difficult to see how the craft unions may have got that impression. In the early 'sixties, Briginshaw publicly declared that he was 'sick' of demarcation disputes in the industry. And in the wake of the general Labour party commitment at that period to industrial efficiency and modern management techniques, his arguments for removing the barriers against unskilled workers in the machine-room (echoing the Isaacs quotation with which I began the chapter) tended to be based more on the need for rationalisation than on justice. As a result it sounded much like the arguments managements were also using.

Moreover, it is true that in general many managers and journalists feel more sympathy with NATSOPA than with the craft unions, again because of their recognition of the frustrations that must attend an assistant who can never be promoted. Since the industry's white-collar employees are all NATSOPA, managers and journalists are also more used to working with them (junior and middle managers at least will themselves usually be NATSOPA members): and, whereas it is pretty rare for a craft official to 'change sides', it has been fairly common practice for companies to hire NATSOPA FoCs as personnel managers.

Superficially, therefore, NATSOPA and managements had much in common – if not enough to lead to an actual conspiracy, at least enough to make the craft unions' suspicions understandable. Objectively such an alliance could only have been based on a deep misunderstanding: that a healthy industry can ever be based on the centralist and dictatorial approach of NATSOPA (even if its overt left-wing political stance is ignored) is highly unlikely. While the craft unions' defence of their status and position may have led to irrationalities in the production system, their basic attitudes and motivations seem much more attuned to the industry's basic needs.

Something of this shows through in the history of the attempts at union amalgamation in the 'sixties. It may have been sadly overdue, but in the wake of the 1962 Royal Commission the various remaining craft unions (with the sole significant exception of SLADE) joined to-gether into the NGA without a great deal of trouble. Given the loose and autonomous structure of the craft unions, it was not too difficult (though I would not want to take any credit away from the people who carried it through) to associate them in the equally democratic organisation of the NGA.

Then, shortly afterwards, NATSOPA and the Paper-Workers announced that they were carrying through an equivalent merger on the non-craft side to form SOGAT. I haven't so far paid a great deal of attention to the former National Union of Paper-Workers (NUPW), which was formed in the same year as NATSOPA, and origi-nally collaborated quite closely with it. The NUPW outside Fleet Street followed a different path from NATSOPA, in that it became partly a craft union, particularly among book-binders. In Fleet Street however it steered a parallel path, although it has always been less emotionally hung up than NATSOPA over the craft-non-craft barrier, mainly because its particular area (the warehouse and the distribution of copies) involves no craft workers.

Like NATSOPA however, it has been a highly centralised organisation, with members dependent for their jobs on the approval of the union hierarchy. And it was almost as dominated by its secretary, Tom Smith, as NATSOPA was by Briginshaw. Merging two authoritarian structures, however, by any method other than conquest or take-over, always presents more problems than associating democratic structures (in Europe it has mostly been the authoritarian political groups which have opposed the spirit of the EEC). And SOGAT was no exception.

In the very first place, the merger had a comic element which presaged its eventual fate. It was set up in two 'divisions', one containing former NATSOPA members under Briginshaw, and one containing former NUPW members under Smith. Which, while hardly promising, was not comic: the comic touch was provided by the fact that the ex-NATSOPA division was called Division 1 and the ex-NUPW division Division A.

Each section kept effectively its own rules and procedures. And, no matter how sick Briginshaw was of demarcation disputes, the significant demarcation between NATSOPA and NUPW jobs remained: printed copies have to be taken off the machine by NATSOPA but bundled and despatched by NUPW. In some highly automated offices, this effectively means that NATSOPA lifts the bundles off the machines on to a table, and the NUPW lifts them off the table on to the vans.

Merging the unions did nothing to get rid of this practice, and indeed after a few uneasy years the unions split again. The join never in fact 'took', and it's difficult to believe that it ever had a chance given the structures of the unions and the attitudes of their leaders. Moreover, while both unions may be categorised generally as 'unskilled', there is actually a deep social differentiation between them which also bodes ill for any merger. Poll any large number of people working in Fleet Street, and the odds are that the majority will agree that the most overpaid and underworked people in the industry (apart from those in the boardroom) are to be found in the warehouse – i.e., they are members of what is now the only remaining division of SOGAT. In particular, members of NATSOPA (whose case against the craft unions is that NATSOPA jobs require just as much skill as NGA ones) are prepared to concede that SOGAT warehousemen are 'really unskilled'. Moreover, there is a kind of priggishness evident in the way NATSOPA, especially the clerical workers, talk about SOGAT that emphasises the divide. Most of the allegations of straightforward industrial sabotage are launched against SOGAT: so too are most of the allegations of corruption in the allocation of casual work. I have heard NATSOPA members describe SOGAT members as 'gangsters', and had it suggested to me that that was the real reason the unions split up again. Whether that is true or not, the general attitude of superiority displayed by NATSOPA vis-à-vis SOGAT leaves nothing but pessimism as a reaction to the possibilities for re-amalgamation.

The attitude is of course parallel to that displayed by the craft unions to NATSOPA itself. I was even assured privately by one senior official of the NGA that, irrespective of the craft status question, the NGA and NATSOPA would never bring off a merger because the NGA would never accept the way NATSOPA kept its books. But perhaps of more interest to anyone trying to think of future developments in the industry is that there is a similar social divide in NATSOPA itself. In a way it's not surprising. At least in Fleet Street, clerical workers in the industry have been members of NATSOPA since the First World War. (Elsewhere in the industry the shop isn't entirely closed.) And especially in recent years, the word 'clerical' has spread out to include varieties of worker never envisaged when the branch was started: workers who in other industries would either not be unionised or might belong to the Association of Scientific, Technical and Managerial Staffs. The category includes not only book-keepers, but chartered accountants: not only salesmen but marketing and market research specialists: if Fleet Street had ever reached as far as industrial engineering, its practitioners would have been NATSOPA members. Probably the only graduate employees in Fleet Street who aren't journalists are in NATSOPA, and are, formally, 'unskilled'.

If such people were to find much in common with the machine-room assistants or the composing-room proof-pullers, it would be surprising. That in fact there is considerable resentment among them against being forced into the union, and a feeling that the union effectively fails to represent their true interests at all is only natural. The chapels that voted against the 1 May strike in 1973 were clerical chapels. They knuckled under to the threat of expulsion, but the resentment remains: a resentment that is mainly directed against the dictatorial nature of NATSOPA, but that has its origins in a sense of misalliance.

Like the craft workers, the orientation of most Fleet Street white-collar workers is essentially bourgeois. Their major aim, at least as far as their working life is concerned, is to practise (and, admittedly, make money out of) their professional skills: to that aim, the projection of socialist principles, defence of the 'blow' system and 'ghost' working, and even advancing the cause of the frustrated machine-room assistants, are all essentially irrelevant. Yet such things remain the major concern of the union.

The apparent solidarity of NATSOPA therefore hides a deep and a widening gulf. The best-disciplined of the Fleet Street unions is at the same time the most unstable, and the only union which, one suspects, faces a serious constitutional crisis in the near future.

I do not know whether that is an optimistic or a pessimistic projection for the health of the industry, except that when the crack comes it is likely to provoke a short-term crisis of some gravity. The only thing that could stop it happening would be of course a prior realignment or merger of NATSOPA and perhaps SOGAT with the craft unions: however, the chance that this can happen, given the incompatible institutions and the inherently antagonistic attitudes of the two sides, seems remote.

11
Journalists

One of the more surprising results of the 1962 Royal Commission on the Press was that the National Union of Journalists began to think. That may seem an uncharitable remark: but it was made to me by a national officer of the NUJ. His point was that only in preparing their evidence for the Commission, and in reviewing other parties' evidence, was it sharply brought home to the union high command just how far behind the other unions the journalists had slipped in terms of both pay and conditions. It was only then that they began to lay serious plans to put the matter 'right': plans that were to pay off handsomely in material terms towards the end of the decade.

Until the early 'sixties, the NUJ had always been a weak union, not merely in Fleet Street terms, but in comparison with many unions in other industries. To begin with, it had no effective control over entry to the profession (temperamentally, I don't think I can avoid calling it that, though I am aware it will lead to raised eyebrows in some circles, and horse-laughs among the craft unions). Employers were free to hire whoever they liked to write for them.

Normally, too, the union had no way of ensuring that such recruits should join the union after they had arrived. Only in the *Daily Herald*, then the TUC newspaper, was there a fully formal closed shop: elsewhere, only the *Mirror* group operated an effective closed shop. My own record of relationships with the union is probably typical: on *Picture Post* I was recruited by the active FoC; at *The Times* I never came across a union representative, and my membership lapsed; at Beaverbrook newspapers I was re-engaged, though with less keenness; at the *Sunday Telegraph* I got out of touch again; and at IPC, confronted with the need to join some union, I opted to join the Institute of Journalists, mainly, I admit, out of a sense of mischief.

The NUJ therefore had none of the strategic power bastions of either the craft unions or NATSOPA/SOGAT. And worse still, it was unable to guarantee security of employment. Managements were free to dismiss journalists for virtually any reason, subject only to the requirement of a reasonable period of notice (for many years, one month for reporters and photographers, three months for sub-editors and other desk staff, longer in cases where individuals had negotiated special contracts). The union could offer its members and potential members neither entry into a closed profession, nor security against dismissal. While it had negotiated minimum rates with the NPA, they were pretty low (at the end of the 'fifties the minimum was still below £1,000 – considerably less than the average earnings of any of the other Fleet Street unions), especially as overtime payments were specifically ruled out. In any case manage-ments were usually prepared to pay more for competent journalists, sometimes very much more. Even in cases of redundancy or dis-missal, they were frequently prepared to grant more than the union asked for: a case in point was the closure of the magazine *Picture Post*, one of the few humorous aspects of which was the arrival of branch officials at a specially-called NUJ chapel meeting, militantly promising to fight for compensation terms. Unfortunately, the terms they proposed were only half what management had already agreed to give.

Even among its members, the NUJ was something of a joke – an attitude strengthened by a general recognition that the union could never successfully call a strike. There were enough non-NUJ journa-lists around to keep most of the papers going, and no one trusted the mechanical unions to give their support to any cause but their own. (With some justification: as I've already mentioned, as late as 1972 the other unions refused to support a strike by the NUJ against United Press International, the American news agency, in London.) Moreover, many of its members were themselves biased against industrial action. Just after the war, the union had been promised special treatment by the employers if it formally forswore use of the strike weapon. It refused, but only narrowly, and twenty years later there were still many members who believed the refusal to be a mistake, and were inclined to blame the poor position of journalists in the industry on the unnecessarily doctrinaire attitude of its leadership. The NUJ was therefore very much of a toothless organi-sation.

But, in 1962, after mulling over its evidence to the Royal Com-mission, it woke up to just how much that toothlessness was costing it, and began to develop a strategy for gaining power. It is hardly surprising that the strategy leaned heavily on the experience of the other unions – the craft unions in particular. That the position of those unions depended almost entirely on two principles – the closed shop and restriction on entry to the profession – was pretty obvious. And the NUJ determined to follow the example.

As far as entry to the profession was concerned, there was already a useful weapon to hand, which management had indeed had a hand in forging. As far back as before the Second World War, Kemsley Newspapers, then publishers of the *Sunday Times*, the *Empire News* and the *Daily* and *Sunday Graphics*, as well as a chain of provincial newspapers, had inaugurated a journalists' training scheme: in the 'fifties, with management-union co-operation, this had developed into the National Council for the Training of Journalists scheme. Like the Kemsley arrangement, the NCTJ scheme hinged on putting journalists through a kind of apprenticeship on provincial newspapers, lasting basically three years, though university graduates were excused one year.

The similarity to the craft apprenticeship system is probably already apparent. And just as most of a compositor's or pressman's apprenticeship is irrelevant to what he is required to do on a national newspaper, so is most NCTJ training irrelevant to what the journalist is required to do. Moreover, just as the NGA member may qualify without ever having seen a rotary press, so too can the NUJ member qualify without ever having had to face any of the technical requirements of writing, subbing or taking pictures for a daily paper, let alone a national daily.

The situation becomes even more extreme with the recently declared intention of the NUJ that the same scheme should also apply to the training of journalists for radio and television work. The object, officially, is that the scheme should produce people capable of working in any sphere of journalism. At one level it sounds good: at another level, it sounds exactly like the arguments for the craft apprenticeship, and from the point of view of the practical needs of the industry is ridiculous. As ridiculous indeed as if the Army were to insist that all its recruits were to undergo the same course of training, designed to equip them to serve in any sphere of military operations.

It was obviously a sound strategic move for the NUJ to establish the principle that qualification under the NCTJ scheme be made a necessary requirement for the recruitment of any journalists. And in the early years they found managements prepared, albeit shortsightedly, to play along. As has been mentioned, the genesis of the scheme lay with management anyway: Kemsley's were for years given to boasting about their own scheme, even though its contribution to the staffing of their own national papers, especially at senior levels, was in fact minimal. Other groups followed suit, IPC and Beaverbrook going so far as to buy up small groups of provincial newspapers overtly foɪ training purposes. (Ironically enough, they operated in competition, partly at least, in South Devon: they were also, in the relatively prosperous years of the late 'sixties and the early 'seventies, just about the only provincial groups that consistently lost money.)

Presumably, attracted by the public relations aspects of the whole project, managements were prepared to let the left jab through because they didn't see the right hook coming. Of itself, the training scheme posed no serious threat: that only happened when it was coupled with the demand for a closed shop. This demand, cleverly enough, was not put dramatically or suddenly, but gradually, over a series of issues. Thus the practice of paying sports stars to have stories and articles 'ghosted' under their name was attacked: and since it was a pretty indefensible practice anyway, the principle was conceded. Star-name articles, at least in the sports field, now have to be cast in the form of interviews. (*The Sun*, for instance, can start an article 'Don't write off Leeds just because they got off to a poor start in the League. That's the message from Leeds and England striker ALLAN CLARKE.' What it can't do any more is say 'Allan Clarke writes. . . .')

The same principle was then applied to fields other than sports, and, in some papers at least, extended to people who didn't need to have their articles ghosted for them, like Clive Jenkins, general secretary of ASTMS, whom the *Daily Mirror* NUJ chapel stopped from contributing articles to the paper.

In less prominent positions the strategy tended to be to concentrate on individual positions one after another. Thus in the early 'sixties, *Sunday Telegraph* columnist Lionel Birch launched several people into Fleet Street careers via the position of his assistant. But by 1967, he had been constrained to hire only established NUJ members for the job.

Over roughly the same period, the channel whereby many women journalists got into the profession (via a secretary's job in an editorial department) had also been stopped up. And the freedom enjoyed by most picture editors in the early 'sixties to hire or commission whatever photographers they liked, irrespective of union member- ship, also vanished. (There was an interesting example of union- management collaboration involved here. The unionists' main complaint about the position was not that the non-union photo- graphers were being paid too little, but that they were being paid too much – and getting the more interesting jobs. On the first count at least some managements tended to agree, with the result that they collaborated in closing the shop, albeit unconscious of what they were doing.)

By the time managements generally woke up to what was going on, so much ground had been conceded that regaining it was out of the question. Even the Industrial Relations Act didn't help. Though it made formal closed shops illegal – except in special circumstances which didn't apply – and written agreements had to acknowledge the fact, both management and unions were aware that the acknowledgement was a formality with no application to reality.

Some managements did fight at the last ditch. *The Observer* and *The Financial Times* (and maybe some others) hung on to their right to recruit specialist commentators from outside the union, and *The Observer*'s editor-in-chief David Astor remained an outspoken opponent of the closed shop and the restriction of entry to the NCTJ training scheme. Unfortunately, his arguments against it all tended to be rational ones. And, as pointed out in the case of the craft unions' apprenticeship schemes, such arguments have no effective weight.

There is no point in arguing intellectually that the craft apprentice- ship is both irrelevant and harmful in the industry's present circum- stances: most union members already know that. But they also know it is one of the main pillars of their way of life, so they are committed to supporting it nevertheless. The same is true of the NUJ and the training scheme: since its point is not to improve the quality of journalism but to establish the power of the union, it is in vain to argue that it does nothing for the former objective – so long as it does so much for the latter.

That, coupled with the effective closing of the shop, it has estab- lished the union's power, is undeniable. From a take-off point somewhere in the middle 'sixties, journalists' pay began to zoom upwards, more than doubling (in terms of the minimum rate) between 1967 and 1972 – a rate of increase better than any achieved by the other unions. With the exception of some NGA craftsmen, journalists are now better paid than any other of the industry's employees.

This achievement of course required something else beside establishing the twin pillars of power, restricted entry and the closed shop. It also required the adoption of effective tactics: and in the middle 'sixties and after the union proved itself adept in learning from its production equivalents most of the tactics listed in Chapter 7. In particular, in company after company, it concentrated on using the technique of the edition-time chapel meeting – probably the technique that wreaks most damage while risking least loss. But it also benefited immensely from that attitudinal weakness in management which will be explored in the next chapter. So used has management become to being in a one-down position against the unions that it had no heart in it for a fight against a new opponent. One of the NUJ's major advantages therefore was the fruit of the years of success of the other unions.

It needed that, because, objectively, it still has several weaknesses compared to the position of the other unions. For instance, the power to dismiss incompetent journalists is still not seriously challenged. In contrast, all craft workers are by definition competent, while with NATSOPA and SOGAT the question of dismissal no longer arises. With competence largely a matter of subjective judgement, the position of the journalists is still relatively insecure. (Especially since journalists, unlike doctors, solicitors and teachers, are still ready to recognise that some of their colleagues are incompetent.)

There are usually several allegations of victimisation sackings of journalists current at any time in Fleet Street, whereas in the last few years I have only heard of two in NATSOPA (one of those in fact from a news agency, and the other from an off-Fleet Street magazine printers), and none at all in the other unions. It is probably significant however that each of those allegations has been made by ultra-left-wing members of the NUJ, with, as often as not, the accompanying allegation that the dismissal was connived at by the official NUJ hierarchy. (That charge was also made in the press agency NATSOPA case.) While the allegations tend to be made by the left wing, it isn't always true that the people sacked were themselves left-wing. In fact, of the three I have met personally, none are any more left-wing than the middle-of-the-road Labour party. But it is true that they were all engaged in organising unofficial industrial action, that they

F

were all subsequently sacked (one not from his main job, but from his Saturday regular engagement on a Sunday sports desk), and that in each case the local NUJ chapel stood passively by. Which obviously makes considerable ammunition for the militant minority which tends to make itself felt more by its skills in self-advertisement than through its numbers.

Off-duty anyway, that minority is ready to admit that the massive majority of the union, and not just the hierarchy, are far from being highly committed politically, let alone sufficiently militant – no matter how much their militancy may have increased, in the eyes of management and the outsider, over the last decade.

There is an apparent contradiction involved here. For it is obvious that the union would not have made the advances it has made were journalists not prepared to join it, support it, and engage in whatever industrial action proved necessary: in other words, to be militant. On the other hand, it is equally obvious from talking to a reasonably wide spectrum of journalists that their political views are at least as widely spread as those of the population at large (though probably more knowledgeable and more cynical). Certainly there are relatively few militant socialists among them: maybe a few more than in the 'fifties, but probably a few less than in the 'thirties.

But the example of the craft unions, from whom the NUJ has learned so much, helps to explain the contradiction. For NUJ militancy is fairly soundly based in bourgeois capitalistic self-interest. This may not be true of their leaders, but it is certainly true of the supporters from whom they derive their power. The aim of the NUJ membership has nothing to do with political ideology: it has everything to do with getting themselves as high and secure a source of income as the production workers.

To anyone who knew Fleet Street fifteen years ago and has been out of touch since then, that statement may sound a little odd. For it was once upon a time true, and is not merely a myth, that Fleet Street journalists, no matter how much they may have been tempted by high earnings, placed no great value on security as a motivator. At least outside *The Times*, and perhaps *The Daily Telegraph* (where anyway security was a matter of keeping in with the management) some sense of glamour, of involvement, of knowing more than the next man, of companionship, of occasional excitement and frequent urgency, indeed of sheer vocation, had more to do with keeping journalists at their job than security. Indeed, for most, security would probably have seemed incompatible with their more basic aims.

But the intervening decade and a half have seen a comprehensive (if I knew a better word I'd use it) bourgeoisification of the journalists' world. Nothing is absolute, of course, but it is certainly a duller place. It is probably less due to changes in the personal attitudes of the people who have worked through it than it is to differences in the kind of people coming into the industry, their background and values (maybe even to deglamorise Fleet Street as a career since the arrival of television). But anyone returning to the industry now after a long period away will tend to look in vain, for instance, for many of the extended drinking sessions that were the usual aftermath of a day's work (he will even, significantly, look in vain for many of the pubs). The old friends he will still find in their usual place will probably have much the same wistful tone as they repeat: 'Used to be they'd all finish their stories, then come on over here for a couple of hours, half-hoping something else might turn up. Now all they think about is finishing their stories in time to catch the train home. And all they talk about is how they can pay off the mortgage.' A biased viewpoint, but with some undoubted truth in it. And a truth that goes some way to explaining the change of heart of the NUJ. Moreover, while they were coincidental, a couple of other things (one event, and one trend) have worked to reinforce the same change. The event was the 1965 budget which for the first time made entertainment expenses not allowable against tax, and which was followed by a general tightening up on journalists' expenses. The same thing happened in other industries of course, but probably in few other places had people been so dependent on topping up their salaries via the expense account as journalists were.

In addition, from the middle 'sixties onwards there was in Fleet Street a general trend away from covering many overseas or provincial stories in a lavish way from the home office. To save money, most if not all papers began covering fewer stories, sending fewer people on them, or using local 'stringers' at the expense of staff men. It made for economy, but it also knocked out one of the props by which many journalists were supporting themselves. It also helped to demoralise the industry, not only from the point of view of recruits, but for those already in it. You no longer joined a newspaper to see the world: and if that was the reason you had joined it, you were likely to start feeling frustrated.

For both these reasons, higher basic salaries became a necessity, just as the emotional bias of many people was swinging towards their greater inherent security. (Obviously there may have been a great deal of push-pull feedback involved here: if the people who were in Fleet Street for the fun left because it was getting dull, the ones who stayed would be on average duller.) And more likely to revitalise (or vitalise) the NUJ.

In all, therefore, the modern NUJ lines up very much alongside the craft unions in terms of attitudes, though from the point of view of their own perceptions of status, the NUJ would probably rank itself, socially, educationally, and in terms of contribution made against reward paid, above the craft unions just as they rank themselves above NATSOPA and NATSOPA ranks itself above SOGAT (while SOGAT seems relatively unworried by the situation). But there are a couple of significant differences between the middle-of-the-road NUJ position and that of the average craftsman. Strikingly, the NUJ on the whole disparages management rather less than the craft unions do. Typically, the craft unionist sees management in Fleet Street as straightforwardly incompetent: NUJ members are much more likely to credit management with intelligence or cunning, and at least with knowing what they are trying to do. This is partly a reflection of the general air of awe with which Fleet Street, in its editorial columns, views commercial processes and those who mastermind them. Effectively the national newspapers have become used to treating business as another branch of the sports/entertainment area. That not only means treating balance sheets, profit and loss accounts and share prices as a kind of running score sheet (an approach that many businessmen of course are perfectly happy to follow): it also means singling out successful personalities, and treating them with much the same respect as the racing writers treat Lester Piggot, say, or the soccer writers used to treat Sir Alf Ramsey. Unavoidably, it also means periodically overblowing an undeserved reputation, and then taking it apart again once the brass feet have been exposed. But in spite of that, there remains the feeling that businessmen have arts and skills of their own which journalists cannot acquire and do not fully understand. (I'm talking about the general run of journalists, not the City specialists, who tend to take a more cynical view, at least outwardly: the history of Press coverage of, say, Pergamon Press even in the specialist areas indicates however that much the same phenomenon can overcome the specialists too).

Internally, much of that attitude shows itself in the view journalists take of their own managements: thus, the allegation that *The Times* (or at least Thomsons) profited immensely from the sale of Printing House Square came to me first from journalists. Some craft union members were prepared to hawk it around for propaganda purposes, but that has nothing to do with their believing it. The point about the journalists was that they believed it. (And that was ironical, since *The Times* management had bent over backwards to explain the progress of the move through their recently inaugurated series of consultative meetings with journalists. Still, no matter what the true motives, those meetings are still viewed with much suspicion as propaganda devices: journalists are fully as eager to see events as public relations exercises as managements are concerned to exploit them that way.)

This particular respect for 'management' skills has a further, and harmful, effect on the senior levels of the editorial hierarchy, but this will be postponed to the next chapter. No matter how they see themselves, I prefer to treat those responsible for managing journalists as managers rather than as journalists.

The other major difference from the craft unions arises from the journalists' rather special concern with editorial policy. As I've pointed out, to their credit the craft unions rather pride themselves on their neutrality towards editorial policy: and while NATSOPA doesn't take exactly the same view, at least whatever pressures it has exerted have tended to be concerned with things affecting its own union.

Even so, journalists' concern with editorial policy is essentially unorganised. For most journalists, the prime concern is with their own individual freedom to write what they themselves want in the way they want to, not to set up some kind of co-operative control system. Most are intelligent (and of course egoistic) enough to realise that participative control is still control, and that, on the whole, it is easier to persuade an editor than a committee. Perhaps oddly, this even appears to be true of most members of the left-wing. At least several acknowledged left-wingers will confess to not having given the matter very much thought: they automatically think and talk in terms of one-man editorship: even in advocating 'socialist' solutions to the editorial problem, their main concern is to 'democratise' ways of picking the editor.

Still, I defined editorial matters as being outside the scope of this book, tempting though they may be: there is plenty of material already available, notably, as far as union/editorial relationships are concerned, in Charles Wintour's *Pressures on the Press*. From my own point of view it is more relevant to switch to the other side of the fence, and consider the attitudes of Fleet Street management.

12
Managers

Fleet Street, with somewhat less justification than Gaul, is traditionally divided into three parts. It consists of those people who are
concerned with what goes into the paper, those who are then
concerned with producing and distributing it, and those who are
concerned with making money out of the operation. Generally
and traditionally, the term 'management' is reserved for the third
category. In terms of the definitions used in outside industry, that
of course is a confusing misuse. It excludes from 'management' a
fairly large number of people who in standard terminology ought
to be included – notably editors and departmental editors. And it
includes a large number of people who ought to be excluded:
advertising salesmen, clerks and book-keepers, and so on. Even the
vocally left-wing section of the NUJ tends, interestingly and surprisingly, to make the same misidentification: for them, anything
but a production or editorial job is 'management', no matter how
little managerial responsibility it may carry.

In writing about Fleet Street, it's only too easy to carry the
confusion over. However, for the purposes of this chapter, I will be
trying to use terms in the way in which they are generally used in
outside industry. That is to say, by 'managers' I only mean people
who are responsible for the work of others; and within that I
include 'editorial managers', though since as a group their attitudes
tend to be different from other managers, I will be mainly considering
them at the end of the chapter. It is also worth making clear at the
start that the concept of the 'middle manager' in general use to
indicate those between board level and front-line management, is
almost inapplicable in Fleet Street. This is partly because there are
simply precious few middle managers. Enterprises are so small, and
the amount of 'managerial' authority that has been arrogated
by the unions is so large, that the average front-line manager
reports to someone who probably reports directly to the chief
executive.

In some of the large corporations, like IPC and Thomsons, of course, the 'senior' management, including the board, would by normal standards be classified as 'middle' in that they report to divisional or group executives higher up the organisation. But, on the whole, the people in that position tend to have assimilated most of the attitudes of their opposite numbers in the smaller companies. If one's concern is with attitudes therefore there is little point in distinguishing between the categories.

Effectively there are only two groups involved: 'senior' managers who, whether they are called directors or not, are practically speaking at board level; and 'junior' managers who report to them, and themselves are directly responsible for controlling operatives of one kind or another.

Outside, perhaps, the editorial departments, 'junior' management, thanks to several factors, is itself of no great importance. Partly, it arises from the strength of the unions, and their habit, already described, of insisting on dealing directly with the 'top'. If all major decisions and most minor ones are dealt with by direct negotiation between unions and senior management, and if fathers of chapels reserve the right to go to senior management on any issue they choose, the role of the junior manager is effectively debased to that of an intermediary message-carrier, and, perhaps, quality-controller. The effect is heightened by the readiness of senior managements to accept this position, itself due to their general unwillingness to delegate responsibility for sensitive decisions: an aspect of the timidity I've already mentioned and will be coming back to. And, finally, the sheer fact that most junior managers are members of the same unions as the people they are responsible for (even if their membership may have been temporarily suspended) both formally weakens their position and gives them a conflicting set of loyalties. With the power balance in Fleet Street the way it is, that conflict is more often than not resolved (from the company's point of view) in the wrong direction. Most front-line managers in the industry both talk and behave more like senior members of the union than like representatives of management. It is a phenomenon which is encouraged by the lack of trust in them usually shown by senior management: and it is also of course a phenomenon which both increases and justifies that lack.

The impotence these factors lead to not surprisingly, and not unfairly, manifests itself in the general lower-management attitude that, whatever else ails the industry, it isn't their fault. Talking to them, it usually becomes evident that they have the same kind of personal dedication to the industry that is also common among the craft unions, journalists and some sections of NATSOPA. But it isn't linked to any impulse to do anything about its troubles: instead there is only concentration on avoiding short-term problems, on getting the blocks ready for tonight's paper, on ensuring that print quality is adequate, that formes go into the foundry on time, and so on. Each night's production is a little like a party game of passing on the hot potato. The only interest is in getting the work out of one department and into another, so that if anything goes wrong it will be someone else's fault.

Magnifying this effect is the fact that for the vast majority of lower management (again, excepting perhaps the editorial departments) there is no visible career structure within the industry (or, indeed, outside it). In general, there is not even any possibility of rotating jobs, of moving from one department to another as a stepping stone to higher things: virtually the whole motivating effect that in most industries is inherent in the management hierarchy is missing. Largely, this is the result of craft structuring: as long as the 'printer' is in effect the senior compositor, and the process overseer is simply the senior SLADE craftsman, mobility is unlikely. But it is also worsened by the way in which the industry tends to recruit its senior managers.

As the unions see it, selection of senior management in Fleet Street is largely nepotistic, even in those cases where family dominance doesn't make the most responsible positions an automatic inheritance. If nepotism, taken literally, is too strong a word, at least the firm union belief is that the main criterion for suitability for senior management is class membership. And the second criterion is willingness to flatter and fawn. Much the same charge is also launched by lower level managers. It was not a union member but a manager who told me that the chief handicap his managing director had was that he always acted as if he was 'born to rule', and extended that to say 'that's the trouble with all of them'. He, incidentally, not only has some thirty years' experience working in Fleet Street but also works for a managing director who doesn't belong to any of the industry's 'families' and tends to pride himself on the openness of his management style and the lengths to which he goes to achieve consultation.

Possibly the union belief that the usual way to get a senior manage-
F*

ment job in Fleet Street is either to be born to it, or to know someone who has a friend, is coloured by the knowledge that this is about the only way to get some craft apprenticeships. Nevertheless, it is difficult to escape the conclusion that there is something in the charge, on most papers at least. The areas from which senior management are recruited are certainly limited, much more so than in the general run of industry, and family interests still control most of the industry: family and social ties can certainly be a powerful factor in influencing appointments. It is difficult indeed to see some appointments in any other light.

The only Fleet Street group not controlled by a family or a trust is IPC, and the managerial picture is indeed different at IPC: even though it too until 1968, whatever the shareholding situation, was in practice controlled by Cecil King (a Harmsworth) as if he were the proprietor. The major difference at IPC in the past has been that it had overseas operations, particularly in West Africa, that it could and did use as a managerial training ground. So many managerial appointments were made from the ex-West African staff that in the late 'sixties it became known as the 'Nigerian Mafia'. While as a practice it may also have had a kind of nepotistic appearance, it nevertheless had the advantage of ensuring that recruits had worked their way up through the production and general management ladder: something which is rare elsewhere in the Street.

Much the commonest road to general management responsibility, apart from family ties, is the advertising department – yet another reflection of the importance Fleet Street gives to selling advertising. In fact there is at least one instance of a managing director being recruited directly from an advertising agency. The only other source tends to be recruitment from the editorial side, but that again has particular characteristics I will be considering later. Virtually unknown is recruitment from outside the industry altogether, except for occasional non-executive board appointments. A major exception of course was the appointment of Alex Jarrett from the Civil Service as managing director of IPC, then as chairman of the Newspaper Division. But that aberration (a potentially healthy one) from the normal pattern, was much more bound up with IPC's position in the Reed International group than it was with any attempt to alter the situation in newspaper management, as was made evident when Jarrett replaced Sir Don Ryder as Reed chairman. Bringing in people 'from outside' is sometimes talked about; but on

closer definition it normally turns out to have meant bringing someone from another paper, or, more extremely, from the provinces or
from advertising.

In the circumstances, it is hardly surprising that attitudes do not
vary very much from company to company across the industry. Even
between publicly and privately owned companies the differences
are slighter than might be imagined – certainly front-line managers
and staff who have worked in both sections find it hard to determine
any difference. One labour relations specialist with experience of
both cast around for several minutes before finally coming up with
the one difference he could see: 'I suppose,' he suggested, 'that if it
had not been a public company, the *Daily Mirror* building would
not have been built.' What he meant was that, if the *Mirror* board
had been spending its own money it wouldn't have put so much
into an expensive status symbol. But one can't be sure. *The Times*
did, even before it was bought by Thomsons. The complex of factors
that, as Parkinson described years ago, lead to the building of a
new headquarters as the final fling of an empire in decline strikes
pretty indiscriminately.

In general, even appointive chief executives and 'board' members
behave as they would expect tycoons to behave. Indeed, it is not
unreasonable of them to ape entrepreneurial behaviour, since Fleet
Street has yet to find any other model apart from the entrepreneurial
one on which to run a successful newspaper. From Northcliffe's
Mail through Beaverbrook's *Express* and King's (and Cudlipp's)
Mirror to Murdoch's *Sun*, all Fleet Street's great success stories
have been built around brilliant individuals who either owned their
paper or behaved as if they did.

In such a situation it is only to be expected that standards of
management education and training, compared to those in industry
at large, should be low. Commenting on the fact, the EIU report in
1966 exempted from the criticism IPC and Thomsons, but, at least
as far as IPC was concerned, they seemed to have been misled,
perhaps from talking to too many optimists at Group headquarters.
The report stated, with regard to the *Daily* and *Sunday Mirrors*:
'The selection and training of managers is planned and organised
at IPC Group level', but to anyone actually involved at the time that
assertion cannot be anything but comic. IPC did make some progress
in developing Group-organised management training: it did nothing
at all in selection. And the newspaper companies made far less use

of central facilities than the others, even absolutely, let alone in relation to manpower.

But while the standard of training in the industry is low, it is perhaps not too unreasonable that it should be. It is generally true that if there is no training for the boss there might as well not be for anyone else (at least, that's an exaggeration but there's something in it). And it is probably even truer in Fleet Street, where the 'boss' tends to play an active day to day role in running things.

This general lack of training is possibly a cause of some of the industry's troubles, but, at a deeper level, it is rather more interesting as a symptom of some of the attitudes which underlie the problems. After all, in the 'sixties anyway most of the industry could have afforded it; and indeed from the time the Industrial Training Act started to bite on the industry in 1969, it even became relatively cheap. Once you were handing over 1 per cent of payroll to the training board, you needed a fairly powerful motive not to get some of it back by organising training, even if you thought it irrelevant, which was probably the handiest overt reason for rejecting it.

The belief that outsiders, be they trainers or consultants, can't help the industry found its most telling expression (at least the most telling I know of) in the evidence given to the 1962 Commission by the proprietors of the later-killed *News Chronicle*. They were asked some special questions, one of which was: did they ever 'seek the assistance of general management-consultants?' They answered, with, one imagines, perfectly straight faces: ' "General Management Consultants" is presumably understood as applying primarily to production and distribution. In both spheres it has not been a matter of discovering where economies could be made but in getting them accepted by the operating staff. This is primarily a psychological problem and to have handed it to outside experts might have had fatal results.'

From the assumption that 'general management' means production and distribution down to the assertion that death is better than risking a fatal disease, this paragraph is about as condensed a collection of nonsense as it is possible to imagine. Yet the thing is not that it is incredible, but that it is almost predictable, that it is only too easy to imagine the same reply being made today, and that there are undoubtedly many people in the industry who will find it perfectly acceptable. After showing the passage to people, I've even had conversations that went something like:

'What's wrong with that?'

'It's nonsense.'

'How is it nonsense?'

'Well . . . for one thing, it says they didn't have any problems in the areas they're specialists in and know a lot about, so they didn't call in consultants there. But they did have problems in areas they haven't had any training in and therefore couldn't see any solution to . . . so they didn't dare call in consultants there either.'

'I don't blame them. You see, what their real problem was . . .'

That's the point at which I give up arguing.

Insularity of this kind, which refuses to accept outside help even in fields where the outsider may have well-defined specialist skills otherwise unavailable, is usually symptomatic of one thing: fear. Or, to use a politer word, insecurity. I can see no reason why that diagnosis should not equally apply to Fleet Street. It is after all borne out by other things. I've already mentioned the industry's automatic adoption of a one-down attitude against the advertiser. An interesting example of it came when the NPA not long ago tried to organise a joint meeting between the papers and the IPA over the question of monitoring mail-order advertising (to check for frauds). The IPA representatives were eager enough: the newspapers turned down the suggestion since, as one put it: 'They'll only turn down anything we suggest, anyway.'

The unnecessary (and suspicion-creating) secrecy with which most companies try to veil their non-newspaper operations, especially in property, is essentially another fear reaction. So too, probably, is the way that the newspapers immediately and virtually automatically conceded the palm as a news-reporting medium to television. And timidity vis-à-vis the unions goes back a long way.

Indeed the NPA itself was born out of timidity. In 1906, the newspapers were still members, in common with other printing establishments, of the Master Printers' Association. Then in June the London Society of Compositors sent a strike notice to the MPA, calling among other things for a 48-hour week and an 8-hour overtime limit. The day before strike ballot papers were due to be issued however, the London Society of Compositors 'received a communication from a body of newspaper proprietors, inviting the Society to a meeting at which no representative of the MPA would be present'. (Quotation from the official history of the LSC). At the meeting, the newspaper employers gave way, and the union agreed in future to treat with the newspapers as a separate organisation. The NPA was born.

Timidity towards the unions doesn't only manifest itself when industrial action is actually taken or threatened. The reluctance of newspapers to write about the industry's labour problems has already been mentioned. But there was a slightly amusing instance arising out of the May Day strike of 1973. I have mentioned that two NATSOPA chapels voted against taking part (which was not mentioned in the papers of course). One went as far as attempting to contact management to tell it of the vote, and, presumably, seek some support. But they needn't have bothered. All the company's labour relations staff were, tactfully, away.

The way the industry concentrates on competition within itself is again a probable symptom of an essential timidity. Ask a newspaperman, editorial or 'management', who his rivals are and at least nine times out of ten he'll name the newspapers that have similar editorial appeal. He won't say television, magazines or books. Some years ago, John Hughes, a director of the advertising agency Hobson Bates, upbraided a conference of IPC executives for the fact that whenever anyone tried to sell him space they only did it by pointing out how much better their paper was than the others. They never sold against television: they only fought for the crumbs that television left over.

More recently, shortly after Frank Rogers became director of the NPA, he determined to try to emulate the example of the American newspapers and magazines, which have special joint bureaux designed to sell newspaper or magazine advertising as such. There was some initial enthusiasm from the specialist advertising directors, which certainly ran to organising a visit to the United States in January 1973, to study how the bureaux operated. The enthusiasm lasted for a while, but then things began to drag. Finally, News International and Beaverbrook withdrew (on the overt grounds that the salary required for someone to co-ordinate a programme was too high) and the enterprise, unavoidably, collapsed.

The main reason for concentrating on fighting the devil you know is that you're frightened of the devil you don't. The second is of course that you don't trust the one you know not to stab you in the back. Undoubtedly both reasons affect Fleet Street. You don't raise your advertising rate to match television increases, because you accept you're not as big a draw as television. You certainly don't raise your advertising rate unless other people raise theirs. And even if they agree to raise theirs, you don't raise yours because you don't trust them not to give covert discounts.

Similarly, you don't fight the unions because you're scared of them, on an individual basis. And you don't fight them jointly because you don't trust anyone else to stand by you: at least you don't trust everybody to stand by you.

So collaboration goes by the board, and those national union leaders I've met continue to gloat over the employers' disunity, which at least in their eyes, is the key advantage they have.

What is difficult to account for is why this kind of timidity affects Fleet Street so uniformly. It is contagious, of course, in that managers like other people tend to adopt the habits of the community they join. But something has to get it started. And as far as I can see there are two possible causes.

One is that the Fleet Street manager, unlike virtually every other Fleet Street worker, is insecure in his job. He can be fired. In any crunch position, against the unions, the advertisers, or whatever, he is like a man playing poker against someone with a much bigger bankroll. He can afford neither to bluff, nor to call the other's bluff. Since he has everything to lose, and his opponent, usually, has very little – or appears to – he concedes. And he concentrates, specifically, on doing the short-term job in hand, avoiding trouble, and as far as possible passing the buck.

The second reason is possibly realisation by most Fleet Street managers that they are, by the standards they imagine the rest of industry to have, essentially not very competent. They tend to be aware of their lack of knowledge and training, to be at least half in agreement with the standard union charge: 'You don't have to be good at anything to be a manager.' The only thing they have to counter this feeling is their specialist knowledge and skill in their own areas: so they concentrate on those (again focusing attention on the short-term job in hand) and on competing with the people who have the same skills and the same limitations – their opposite numbers on rival papers.

The obvious answer to such a situation, apart from massive re-training, is a sizeable injection of outside managers. But since the general insecurity extends to the top of the organisation, such a solution is virtually impossible: in fact, just such an injection is one of the things people are afraid of.

If defensiveness and timidity are endemic among Fleet Street managers, they are probably even more deeply rooted among the category of managers I have saved till last: editorial managers. In general, editors avoid the tag 'manager', which wouldn't matter so much if they were willing to accept the reality: whatever they call themselves they are what the rest of the world calls managers. It might then be easier to get them to accept that management training and skills are relevant to their roles. (Some do, but they don't always have encouraging experiences as a result. The editor of one national newspaper a few years ago became interested enough in the subject to be reading Douglas McGregor's book *The Human Side of Enterprise* – a highly relevant piece of reading for any editor – in his office. But it didn't help his subsequent dedication to self-improvement when his editorial director walked in and said: 'Hello . . . what're you doing reading that rubbish?')

Having battled against it for some years, I have little doubt that the attitude is a defensive rationalisation, magnified by the fact that most products of the editorial organisation tend to be, if not innumerate, at least unhappy dealing with mathematics, even of the elementary kind used by accountants. Stepping out of the role he knows immediately makes the ex-journalist insecure: a feeling that is heightened by the need to deal with 'management' people, the very people he has been conditioned during his years in the profession to mistrust. After a working life spent as one of 'us' against one of 'them' it isn't easy to bridge the gap. It's even harder when you suspect that 'they' know things you don't – and can't admit you don't.

To some extent too there is a general feeling that 'management' necessarily involves 'profit-seeking', 'controlling costs', 'money-grubbing' and suchlike undesirable activities which are a contradiction of their editorial role.

For some of the NUJ militants, anyone accepting an editorial chair is already automatically a traitor to the cause. Probably not many journalists would go as far as that: but barriers tend to go up against any journalist who actually moves into a 'management' job. The sense of distance and separation is equally felt by the person making the move, no matter how conscious he himself may be of the fact that economic efficiency is desirable in any operation, whatever its mission. Undergoing management training is perhaps not so bad as actually taking a management job. But it has a similar smell. Which is one of the major tragedies of the Fleet Street situation. For, if one looks around for some source from which to find the people who might help to change things, the most obvious, from the point of view of education, talent and intelligence, is the editorial side. But with attitudes the way they are, that source is permanently untappable.

Appendix: Strangers start here

There are two basic sources of confusion for strangers attempting to study the workings of Fleet Street. One is simply a matter of jargon and technical terms, and is reasonably easy to deal with: the glossary at the end of this section should be a help. The other however is not just a matter of words but of perceptions: it is not a question of the labels being used, but of what is being labelled.

Thus, the term 'management' is used differently in Fleet Street from the way it is generally used in industry – i.e., to refer to people who control the work of others. In Fleet Street the term is used to identify a group of people not usually categorised separately in the general run of industry: those responsible for making money. In industry in general that is supposed to be a concern of everyone – at least everyone except perhaps shop-floor workers. But the Fleet Street world view identifies three major categories of people in the industry, irrespective of their positions in what other industries would call the management hierarchy.

One of these categories is 'editorial': the people responsible for providing the text and the pictures that go into the paper. The second is 'production': those responsible for printing and publishing and distributing it on schedule. And the last is 'management': those responsible for (and interested in) making money out of the whole process.

Thus, in the Fleet Street idiom, the news editor, though he may have some dozens of people working under him, is not a manager, and he may well resent being called one. On the other hand, anybody working in, say, the advertising department is 'in management', though he may be simply a salesman.

That there should be a differentiation between editorial and management on these lines may not be too surprising: a similar distinction exists for instance in hospitals between medical and administrative staff. What is easier to miss, and more difficult to accept, is that there is a similar dichotomy between 'production' and 'management'. It does not (as might seem at first sight) parallel the traditional cleavage between production and sales in most industries. There the clash is between two different approaches to making profits: maximising revenues and minimising costs. In Fleet Street however the distinction is more fundamental. The production worker and the production manager both see their major task as getting the papers printed and into the readers' (or at least the wholesalers') hands. That is where their craft and their vocation lie: economy is rarely if ever a consideration. One could perhaps push the hospital analogy a little further: in which case the parallel to the newspaper's production staff is not the administration, but the nursing staff. If the editor is the senior consultant, the production manager is the matron. Notably, in some departments, the process department and the reading-room for instance, the 'production' worker is likely to see part of his role as the correction of editorial error: again something that has its analogies with nursing.

'Management' is therefore in Fleet Street terminology a description of a function – a group of people with an assumed common interest – rather than the upper levels of a hierarchy. Not only is management assumed to have a common interest: it is also assumed to have different social habits and a different value system from either the editorial group or the production group. Generally speaking, these assumptions are true.

Less confusing perhaps, but still important to remember, is that all the newspaper companies with which this book is concerned are essentially small. Their circulations may be massive, their financial standing sometimes impressive (in their heyday the two *Mirrors* were making something like £5–6 million in profits each year), and some of them may belong to major industrial groups. But in all of them the 'bosses' are close to the front line. In many cases – *The Sun* and the *News of the World*, the *Telegraphs*, the *Mail* and the *Expresses* – that boss is still the proprietor. But even in the others, where by general industrial standards the controlling executives would be middle managers, they are still treated as, and tend to look on themselves as, main board directors if not proprietors.

None of them are separated from the operative worker by more than two levels of management: levels that anyway tend to be ignored by the unions in day-to-day matters as well as major negotiations.

The best way of introducing the various unions that so dominate the Fleet Street scene is probably to run through the various activities that go into the production of a newspaper, labelling each with its union allegiance. It is equally a way of introducing those activities, and bringing in a few of the more important technical terms.

The main raw material of newspapers is of course information of one kind or another – articles, news stories, publicity handouts, photographs, drawings. Where they consist of words, the generic term is 'copy'. Copy and pictures are either produced by staff (reporters, photographers and artists belong to the NUJ) or flow in from outside. From whatever source it comes, if copy arrives by telephone it is taken down by operators who are members of NATSOPA; other telecommunications media are operated by members of one branch of the NGA (the former Press Telegraphists' union). (This particular disparity occasionally has odd effects – when *The Times* set up a unified telecommunications department in one large room, NATSOPA members occupied one end of it and NGA members the other.)

Received, copy is subbed ('edited' in more usual English) by members of the NUJ; pictures are also selected by NUJ members, though the darkroom where they are developed and printed is manned by NATSOPA. (Another slight oddity is that this does not apply to pictures received by wire or radio, which are developed by NGA operatives. Pictures to be transmitted however are developed by NATSOPA.)

Copy is set in type by compositors who are members of the NGA (the part that used to be the London Typographical Association and before that was the London Society of Compositors), which is checked by other members of the NGA (who used to be in the Association of Correctors of the Press) called 'readers', who read proofs that are called 'pulls'. Readers' assistants are called 'copy-holders' and are members of NATSOPA. The operators who actually make ('pull') the proofs ('pulls') are members usually of SOGAT.

Approximately equivalent to the role of the compositors is that of the process workers who make metal blocks from pictures: they are members of their own union SLADE, which has remained independent of the general move towards merger among the craft unions. (Proofs of blocks are again usually made by SOGAT members.)

Blocks and type are merged into pages by specialist compositors called 'stone-hands' who belong to the NGA. What goes where in the page is supervised by an NUJ member called a 'stone-sub': traditionally he and the stone-hand stand on opposite sides of the 'stone' (the long metal bench on which the pages are made up), so that the stone-hand learns to read type which is the right way up but the wrong way round, while the stone-sub learns to read type the wrong way up but the right way round.

Once the pages are assembled, plates are made from them in the foundry, which is staffed by NGA members who used to belong to the independent stereotypers' union, the National Society of Electrotypers and Stereotypers. The plates are then fitted on to the presses, which are called machines, stand in the machine-room, and are controlled by machine-minders (sometimes called machine managers) who belong to the NGA in all present Fleet Street houses except the *News of the World* where they are NATSOPA. This part of the NGA used to be part of the London Typographical Society, like the compositors, but before that (up to the early 'fifties) was the independent London Machine Managers Society.

As well as the machine-minder, the press is also crewed by four or five assistants, with traditional rather than functional responsibilities, who are considered unskilled and belong to NATSOPA. The most egregious of these is the 'fly-hand' – a job with a title 200 or more years old, and dating back to when sheets had to be removed from the press by hand, as it was operating – that is, 'on the fly'.

As they come off the presses, copies are made into bundles in the warehouse (by members of SOGAT) and distributed in vans (also by members of SOGAT, two to a van).

Besides the editorial and production processes of course, accounts have to be made up, things bought and sold, advertising won, circulation campaigns planned, letters typed and executives' 'phones answered. In some companies anyway, market research has to be done, training programmes organised, planning and control functions carried out and so on and so forth. These jobs are all done by members of NATSOPA, with two exceptions. Directors' secretaries, like directors, are exempt from union membership. And anything electrical or to do with mechanical maintenance is handled by members of the Fleet Street branches of the Electrical Trades Union and the Amalgamated Union of Engineering Workers respectively, the only two unions in the whole picture who have members in industries outside printing and publishing and 'allied trades'.

There exists an association of trade unions called the Printing and Kindred Trades Federation, which is sometimes powerful and sometimes weak and is currently in a waning phase. NATSOPA and

SOGAT sometimes belong to it and sometimes don't: at any given time I hesitate to commit myself on the point. Equally there exists an association of newspaper employers called the Newspaper Publishers' Association. At the moment the *Mirrors* and *The People* do not belong to it.

In detail, the union organisations vary (see Chapters 9 and 10 particularly) but in general they are roughly similar. In each department of the paper, each union will have a 'chapel'; at its head is an elected 'Father of the Chapel' or, briefly, 'FoC'. (In NATSOPA and the NUJ one occasionally meets a 'Mother of the Chapel': none of the other unions have women members in Fleet Street.)

Since this is a more romantic title than 'shop steward', it may not be surprising that the equivalent of a chief convenor (i.e., the senior representative of all the chapels on a particular newspaper) is called the 'Imperial Father'. Between the chapels and the national organisations there is a rather more prosaically named branch level. For the most part, the people working in Fleet Street belong to a London (or, as with the NUJ, a Central London) branch, though NATSOPA, for instance, is split between the London Machine Branch, the London 'Revisers and General Assistants', and the Clerical Branch. How much authority and respect the branch (and national) organisations have varies from union to union – again this is part of the subject matter of Chapters 9, 10 and 11.

It is a complex situation, but at least it is much simpler than it was before the merger of most of the craft unions into the NGA in the early 'sixties: even if it is not so simple as it would have been had not the merger between NATSOPA and SOGAT in the later 'sixties not proved abortive.

With any luck that is enough background for even the stranger to the industry. As the book unrolls, and with the help of the glossary, I can only hope that the stranger can begin to make head and tail of a situation that still from time to time baffles even those brought up in it.

Glossary

BLOCKS The metal plates from which drawings and photographs are reproduced.

BLOW Industry jargon for rest-period. A one-for-one blow system is one in which one hour's work is followed by one hour's rest. In Fleet Street, however, the 'blow' period is frequently worked, and paid for extra at overtime rates.

CHAPEL The smallest unit of trade union organisation: equivalent to the 'shop' in most industries.

CLAUSE IV The article in the constitution of the British Labour party which commits it to the nationalisation of the means of production, distribution and exchange.

COMPOSITOR The craftsman who sets type. Since the late nineteenth century this has mostly been done by keyboard machine, but some large headlines are still hand-set.

FAT Work not done, but paid for. Mostly, the result of advertisers sending in advertisements in the form of blocks (q.v.). The newspapers' compositors are paid as if they had set the type themselves.

FATHER OF THE CHAPEL Local union official, equivalent to shop steward in other industries. Term has been in use for something like 500 years. In the unskilled unions (the only ones with women members) the term 'Mother of the Chapel' is also used where appropriate.

FLY-HAND Assistant whose job it is to remove printed sheets from the press. Nowadays done mechanically, but the fly-hand still sits there.

FOC Father of the Chapel (q.v.)

GHOST WORKING Used to refer to the situation in which actual manning levels are lower than those agreed. The pay of the notional workers is then distributed among those actually working.

HATTERSLEY An early composing machine. Unlike the more successful Linotype and Monotype machines, it required two-man operation.

JOURNEYMAN Craftsman who has 'served his time' as an apprentice, but works for pay (originally by the day – hence 'journeyman' from Fr. *journée*). A 'Master' printer is one who employs journeymen.

LINOTYPE Most successful of the composing machines, which has been more or less standard equipment in newspapers since the late nineteenth century. Ought to have been replaced by more modern technology but has not been.

'LUMP', The difficult to define phrase from the construction industry. 'Working the lump' means hiring out one's services to an employer on a contractual and legally self-employed basis, which has certain legal and illegal tax advantages over working as an employee and having tax deducted at source.

MACHINE Standard industry jargon for the press itself.

MACHINE MANAGER Craftsman who controls the press and, notionally, its unskilled crew. In effect, the quality controller, though he also stops and starts the machine.

MACHINE-MINDER Alternative to MACHINE MANAGER.

NATSOPA National Society of Operative Printers and Assistants (now with 'and Media Personnel' tacked on). The larger of the unskilled unions in Fleet Street, which also includes clerical and managerial personnel. Has routed occasional attempts by the Association of Scientific, Technical and Managerial Staff to get representation in Fleet Street. Once briefly part of SOGAT (q.v.).

NGA National Graphical Association. Result of the early 'sixties merger of most of the craft unions in the industry: compositors, readers, stereotypers, machine-minders, press telegraphists. At the time of writing does not include SLADE (q.v.).

NPA Newspaper Publishers' Association, which changed its name recently from Newspaper Proprietors' Association. The NPA is the trade association of the national daily and Sunday newspapers; there are separate trade associations for provincial newspapers and for periodicals.

NUJ National Union of Journalists – the union to which most British journalists belong.

PROCESS DEPARTMENT Department where 'blocks' (q.v.) are made. For the most part, staff belong to SLADE.

PROOF-PULLER Operative who takes proofs ('pulls') from the type once set. Accepted as an 'unskilled' operation.

SLADE Society of Lithographic Artists, Designers and Engravers. As far as Fleet Street is concerned, the people who retouch photographs and drawings and then make blocks from them. Highly conscious of craft origins and status and so far not amalgamated with anyone. It is worth noting that the artists themselves (and photographers) are members of the National Union of Journalists. Darkroom workers are 'unskilled' members of NATSOPA.

SOGAT Society of Graphic and Allied Trades. Set up in the 'sixties as the merger of NATSOPA and the National Union of Paper and Book-binding Workers, the two unskilled unions. Kept the name when NATSOPA left again.

STEREOTYPING Process of making cylindrical plates from the pages of type. The plates are then mounted on the printing rollers of the press.

Bibliography

Economist Intelligence Unit, *The National Newspaper Industry: A survey*, EIU, London, 1966

Douglas McGregor, *The Human Side of Enterprise*, McGraw Hill, New York, 1960

Royal Commission on the Press, 1948, *Report*, HMSO, London, 1948

Royal Commission on the Press, 1961–62, *Report*, London, 1962

Royal Commission on the Press, *Interim Report*, London, 1976

Keith Sisson, *Industrial Relations in Fleet Street*, Blackwells, Oxford, 1975

Francis Williams, *The Right to Know*, Longmans, London, 1969

Charles Wintour, *Pressures on the Press: An Editor Looks at Fleet Street*, Deutsch, London, 1972

Index